Presented to:

_____

From:

_____

Date:

_____

3ABN BOOKS is dedicated to bringing you the best in published materials consistent with the mission of Three Angels Broadcasting Network. Our goal is to uplift Jesus Christ through books, audio, and video materials by our family of 3ABN presenters. Our in-depth Bible study guides, devotionals, biographies, and lifestyle materials promote whole person health and the mending of broken people. For more information, call 618-627-4651 or visit 3ABN's Web site: www.3ABN.org.

PAUL AND CAROLYN RAYNE

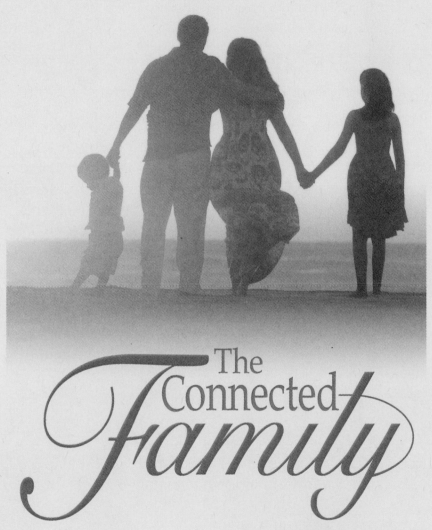

The Connected Family

Pacific Press® Publishing Association
Nampa, Idaho
Oshawa, Ontario, Canada
www.pacificpress.com

3ABN
books

Three Angels Broadcasting Network
West Frankfort, Illinois
www.3abn.org

Cover design by Gerald Lee Monks
Cover design resources from iStockphoto.com
Inside design by Aaron Troia

The authors assume full responsibility for the accuracy of all facts and quotations as cited in this book.

Additional copies of this book are available from three locations:

Adventist Book Centers®: Call toll-free 1-800-765-6955 or visit http://www.adventistbookcenter.com.

3ABN: Call 1-800-752-3226 or visit http://www.3abn.org.

Restoration International: Call 1-888-446-8844 or visit http://www.restoration-international.org.

Unless otherwise noted, Scripture quotations are from The New King James Version, copyright © 1979, 1980, 1982, Thomas Nelson, Inc., Publishers.

Scripture quotations marked NIV are from the HOLY BIBLE, NEW INTERNATIONAL VERSION®. Copyright © 1973, 1978, 1984 by International Bible Society. Used by permission of Zondervan Publishing House. All rights reserved.

Scripture texts credited to NRSV are from the New Revised Standard Version of the Bible, copyright © 1989 by the Division of Christian Education of the National Council of the Churches of Christ in the USA. Used by permission. All rights reserved.

Library of Congress Cataloging-in-Publication Data:

Rayne, Paul, 1965-
  The connected family : simple steps to positive parenting / Paul and Carolyn Rayne.
      p. cm.
   ISBN 13: 978-0-8163-2457-6 (pbk.)
   ISBN 10: 0-8163-2457-3 (pbk.)
   1. Child rearing—Religious aspects—Seventh-day Adventists.
   I. Rayne, Carolyn, 1963- II. Title.
   BV4529.R39 2011
   248.8'45088286732—dc22

                                                                        2010053330

11 12 13 14 15 • 5 4 3 2 1

Dedication

To our parents,
Brian and Barbara Whiting, and Jack and Joy Rayne,
who lovingly poured themselves into our developing lives.
Thank you, Mom and Dad!
And to all parents desiring to see their children enter the
kingdom of heaven.

Table of Contents

Introduction

As parents, we desire to give our children the best. Their happiness during childhood and youth and their future success as adults are important to us. Yet, deep in our hearts, we know our children are not the priorities they should be. Yes, we provide them with material things, but we are allowing our own busyness to steal time and training that are rightfully theirs.

God never intended parenting to be filled with missed opportunities, regrets, and frustrations. Oh, how He longs to make our homes places of joy and places to help our precious children become respectful, obedient, and happy. But for children to develop their potential, parents must learn to do their part!

The Connected Family is a practical twenty-six step program designed to help parents make their children high priorities, lead them to make commitments to God, and teach them the tools for Christian living.

Section 1, chapters 1–13, is dedicated to teaching parents how to win the affections of their children. A solid relationship with our children is the foundation of successful parenting. Without our children's affections, our progress in parenting will be slow and laborious. When we have won our children's hearts, our parenting becomes not only more effective but also the rewarding experience God intended it to be.

The second section, chapters 14–17, builds on the close relationship gained in section 1 and teaches parents how to lead their children to make commitments to follow God.

The third and final section, chapters 18–26, introduces valuable principles that unite the family. It teaches both parents and children how to advance in the practical Christian life.

Each chapter contains an informative reading, a Step Forward section, and a Journal Questions and Answers section. The Step Forward section outlines assignments for each day. The Journal Questions and Answers section gives opportunity to evaluate our progress and journal our thoughts and activities.

The Connected Family is not primarily a book you read. *It is a book you do!* Reading the chapters without wholeheartedly engaging in the activities will not bring maximum results. Remember, we learn to swim in the water, not by standing on the shore!

Each chapter is intended to bring tangible results. You are not left to read long passages of theories and then figure out how to apply them to your parenting. Each chapter is concise, practical, and rewarding for both you and your children.

We recommend you read a chapter each day. If some of the Step Forward assignments take more than a day—and a few of them will—feel free to take extra time to accomplish them before moving on. Some of the Journal Questions and Answers responses will be best recorded after the day's activities or at the beginning of the following day.

We encourage you to go through *The Connected Family* with your spouse, if possible. You will have the best results if you each obtain a copy. Having your own copies will allow both of you to answer the questions and journal your thoughts privately before coming together to discuss what you found and how to practically carry out the latest step. If that is not possible or if you are a single parent, then consider going through this book with someone in a similar situation—perhaps another single parent or a friend. You can encourage each other and share your progress!

Implementing the principles taught in *The Connected Family* will not be easy, but the book will provide you with an opportunity and a challenge to become the parents you have always longed to be. Your children will thank you someday!

SECTION 1

Winning Our Children's Hearts

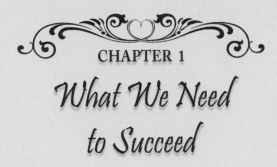

CHAPTER 1

What We Need to Succeed

Whatever your hand finds to do, do it with your might.
—Ecclesiastes 9:10

In 1914, British explorer Ernest Shackleton set sail aboard the *Endurance,* seeking the last unclaimed prize in polar exploration—crossing the Antarctic continent on foot.

As the *Endurance* neared the Antarctic coast, the ship became immobilized in pack ice. Shackleton and his twenty-seven men faced the grim reality that they were trapped. Solid ice surrounded them as far as the eye could see.

Locked in ice, they drifted north for the next ten months. As pressure from the ice increased, the wooden ship twisted and groaned until it tilted at a thirty-degree angle. Shackleton acknowledged the inevitable: what the ice gets the ice keeps. He gave orders to abandon ship. Men, dogs, lifeboats, and supplies were unloaded. A few weeks later, the *Endurance* went down. The crew was now stranded on a giant ice raft in the Weddell Sea, three hundred miles from land.

Shackleton's focus became the survival of *all* his men. His first instinct was to walk across the ice to safety, but he soon realized the utter impossibility of traversing the jagged ice floes with their supplies and boats. They were forced to set up Patience Camp and wait for an opportunity to escape the grip of the ice. As weeks rolled into months, the ice began to break up. The swell of the sea could be felt once more. Five months after being forced onto the ice, the floe on which they were camped broke in two, and Shackleton gave orders to launch the three boats. Elephant Island, one hundred miles to the north, was their destination.

The next seven days at sea were almost unbearable. Bitter cold, along with wild winds and waves that repeatedly drenched the men, threatened to end their miserable existence. It took constant effort to stay afloat. Mind-numbing exhaustion almost extinguished all hope of survival. But finally, for the first time in 497 days, all twenty-eight men set foot on land, the barren and uninhabited Elephant Island.

Knowing there was little chance of ever being rescued from their current location, Shackleton decided to go for help. Taking the largest lifeboat, the twenty-two-foot-long *James Caird*, and five men, he set out to cross some of the roughest seas known to man. This time, their destination was South Georgia Island, an intimidating eight hundred miles away!

On the rough sea, the *James Caird* became dangerously coated with ice, both inside and outside, requiring hours of tedious chipping to keep it afloat. Overcast skies made star-based navigation challenging. But after seventeen days in stormy seas and hurricane-force winds, the *James Caird* miraculously landed on the west coast of South Georgia Island.

They were agonizingly close to their destination. Their goal, a whaling station on the other side of the island, was still twenty-two miles away. With frostbitten feet, Shackleton and two others set off across uncharted mountains. South Georgia's nine-thousand-foot peaks were considered impassable. Glaciers, crevasses, and precipices turned the tired men back time and again. They were forced to descend a steep icy slope just as night was falling. Hacking each step with an ax made progress so slow that they risked freezing to death. The alternative was another incredible risk. The men linked together, forming a three-man toboggan team—minus the toboggan. Not knowing what lay ahead, they hurtled down the slope for a hundred heart-pounding seconds. Their laugher when they landed in a snowbank revealed their relief.

The thirty-six-hour hike finally brought them to the whaling station, where they made rescue plans for the remaining men. Three months later, all twenty-eight men were reunited. Not one was lost.

How does Shackleton's heroic story relate to parenting? While we may not face Shackleton's polar-expedition challenges, it's no easy task to raise children. Ice and wind may not block our progress but plenty of things do. This modern secular world is filled with temptations and difficulties we must learn to recognize and overcome. Like Shackleton, we can lead our children to safety. Not one needs to be lost.

Shackleton's family motto was *fortitudine vincimus,* "by endurance we conquer." In the delicate work of raising children, we will need to add three additional requests to our prayers for endurance. We need to ask God for power, determination, and commitment.

Praying for power

God has more than enough power to carry us through the upcoming weeks of focused parent training. To receive this power, James 4:2 tells us we must pray for it. "You do not have because you do not ask." A simple prayer may be, "Thank You, God, for this opportunity to be a better parent. Give me Your power daily to rise above my old habits and to respond more appropriately to my children. Thank You for answering my prayer. Amen." With God's enabling power in our lives, we can succeed where we have previously failed.

Praying for determination

Shackleton was determined. This same attitude is needed in raising our children. Difficulties will come. We can count on that. Seemingly insurmountable roadblocks will hinder our progress, but God stands ready to fill us with determination. To receive it, we must personally ask God to make it a reality in our lives, and He will!

Praying for commitment

Are you willing to commit the next four to six weeks to your children? This commitment will mean some other pursuits will have to be postponed. Plans may have to be altered. To have the depth of commitment that will make this endeavor a success, we need God's help. For the benefit of our families, we will need the commitment to put aside our individual plans and desires. We will need commitment to overcome our children's possible disinterest and indifference. Again, we must ask God for the commitment needed to achieve our goals. He is willing and waiting to answer this prayer!

Praying for our children

Chapter 15 will guide us in asking our children to make a deeper commitment to Christ; and although we will spend the next couple of weeks working toward this goal, the Holy Spirit is the only One who can change hearts. In addition to praying for power, determination, and commitment, begin praying specifically that each of your children will choose to follow the Lord.

Step Forward

☐ Pray specifically to be filled with God's power, determination, and commitment.

☐ Pray specifically for each of your children by name.

18

Journal Questions and Answers

1. Rewrite Ecclesiastes 9:10 in your own words: "Whatever your hand finds to do, do it with your might."

   _____

   _____

   _____

   _____

   _____

2. Which quality do you feel you need the most—power, determination, or commitment? Why?

   _____

   _____

   _____

   _____

   _____

3. What are the main issues that need to be addressed in each of your children? Did you pray specifically for them and yourself in these areas?

   _____

   _____

   _____

   _____

   _____

Success seems to be largely a matter
of hanging on after others have let go.
— William Feather

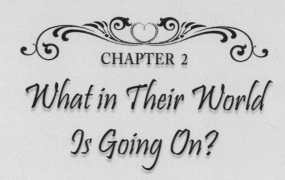

CHAPTER 2

What in Their World Is Going On?

Be diligent to know the state of your flocks, and attend to your herds.
—Proverbs 27:23

When children become interested in activities their parents struggle to relate to, we give the disconnect a name. We say there is a generation gap. It does not happen overnight, and usually it is not the fault of the youth. This difference in values and attitudes often results from the parents' insufficient effort to stay connected to the expanding world of their children. We frequently are not half as interested in our children as we need to be in order to make our parenting successful. Overcommitment in some areas and laziness in others lead us to neglect our children in a variety of ways. Over time, as a natural consequence of our neglect, the children grow away from us and away from our influence. If this pattern is not corrected, eventually our young people will conclude, *Mom and Dad just don't understand. They are from a different age and on a different page.*

Such distancing doesn't have to be our experience. How we connect and stay connected with our children is the object of today's activities. We need to become more observant. We need to know what is going on in our children's world. We need to listen carefully to their conversations. What do they like to talk about with their siblings? What do they discuss with their friends? What topics spark their interest when we engage them in conversation? Once we have an understanding of these things, we will be able to connect with them more intelligently.

Each room in the home will tell us something about our children. We may see their favorite beverages in the refrigerator or notice a new shirt in the laundry; but of all the rooms in the house, their bedrooms will tell us the most about their world. Take a tour of your children's rooms when they are not present. What is on their walls, in their closets, and in their dresser drawers? Ignore the mess for now and take in all the objects. Take time to peruse the books on their shelves and flip through any magazines or other reading material you come across. What type of clothes do they like to wear? If they have a TV, note which channel was viewed most recently. Which DVDs and CDs appear to be their favorites? If they have an iPod or MP3 player, what music or videos have they downloaded? These careful observations will give us valuable insight into their world.

Soon we will begin to see that our children are like twenty-four-hour radio stations. They are constantly transmitting their needs, desires, likes, and dislikes; but only those who are tuned in will receive the signals. Are we receiving the signals our children are consciously or unconsciously transmitting every moment of the day?

Do we know whether our children have any goals or dreams for the future? With younger children, do we know their favorite colors, their favorite foods, their favorite clothes, or their favorite places to go? Who are their closest friends? Who are they spending time with? Do we know who our older children are calling on the phone? Do we know what text messages they are sending and receiving, who they are e-mailing, and who is e-mailing them? Do we know the sites they visit on the Internet, what they have marked for quick access, and their browser history? Who are their friends on Facebook or other social networking sites? Who are they chatting with online? What images are they sending each other? What about the language they are using to describe their world? Is it respectful, or is it filled with slang learned from friends or from what they are watching and reading?

If you have teenagers with access to the Internet or a cell phone and any of this technology is foreign to you, you need to learn about the technology and how teens use it. There is a whole new world out there, and it is our responsibility to be informed about the potential dangers. Begin with a visit to www.internetsafety101.org.

There is another side to observing our children. What do they avoid? What do they dislike? Are they encountering any problems at school? Have they expressed preferences that we have quickly and thoughtlessly criticized?

We should also examine our children's spiritual world. Are they more interested in spiritual things now than a year ago, or are they less interested? Are they maturing in Christ as the years pass, or are they becoming disinterested?

Perhaps you feel disconnected from your children and realize that you have neglected to take interest in their world. Do not be discouraged. It is not too late! This can be the day you begin to become observant, connected parents. Once you do connect with their world, you will find yourselves making all kinds of interesting observations that will help you guide your young people in the days ahead. Remember, working through *The Connected Family* is a process, and becoming more observant is just one step in winning your children's hearts!

Today's chapter has presented many questions that will require some thought to answer. Do not allow yourself to be disheartened; remember yesterday's prayer. By making the effort now to tune it to your children's world, you are closing the generation gap before it has a chance to grow any wider. By being observant and proactive parents, you are doing more good than you realize.

Note: Today is not the day to solve problems; it is a day to simply observe. Refrain from reacting to any findings with negative actions, words, or feelings. Do not confront your children with anything you found disturbing. In later chapters, we will delve into the heart of any issues that may have come to light during your observations. In the meantime, let's put into practice the verse that advises, "Let every man be swift to hear, slow to speak, slow to wrath" (James 1:19).

Step Forward

☐ Pray specifically for God to lead you in your observations.

☐ Without making your motives or activities known, tune in to your children's world today.

☐ Take time to privately compare your observations with your spouse if possible.

Journal Questions and Answers

1. Rewrite Proverbs 27:23 in your own words: "Be diligent to know the state of your flocks, and attend to your herds." Replace *flocks* with the names of your children.

_____

_____

_____

_____

_____

_____

_____

_____

_____

2. What areas of your life have prevented you from connecting with your children? Where have you been overcommitted or lazy? Be honest and specific.

_____
_____
_____
_____
_____
_____
_____
_____
_____
_____

3. What did you find in your children's rooms that surprised you both positively and negatively?

_____
_____
_____
_____
_____
_____
_____
_____
_____

You learn something every day
if you pay attention.
— Ray LeBlond

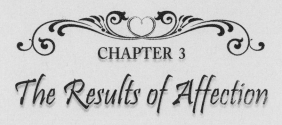

CHAPTER 3

The Results of Affection

Be kind to one another, tenderhearted, forgiving one another,
even as God in Christ forgave you.
—Ephesians 4:32

Yesterday you may have observed things that cause you to be concerned. In later chapters, these issues will be addressed; but in order to obtain a favorable response from our children when we express our concerns, we must first learn the right approach. Immediately attacking the issues is not the best plan. Approaching our children with tenderness will produce more desirable results. Kindness will win children to us; criticism will drive them away. Encouragement draws them in; unnecessarily pointing out their faults pushes them away. We have much to consider before we can effectively address yesterday's discoveries.

Even though we recognize it is not the best method, we often try to improve our children's behavior by correcting their bad habits. We tell them, "Don't do this," or "Stop doing that." We may even resort to that exaggerated accusation: "If I've told you once, I've told you a thousand times." This approach is about as effective as trying to kill a weed by plucking off one or two leaves each day. These leaves, the bad habits of our children, grow slowly at first, but the time comes when more leaves begin to sprout than we can pluck. Once our children are teenagers, the leaves grow so prolifically that many parents find themselves overwhelmed, frustrated, and discouraged. This despair is the result of having the wrong focus! It is not primarily the leaves that we need to address but, rather, the roots of the problem. If we determine, day by day, to win the hearts of our children with kindness, we will be able to keep up with pruning the leaves. However, without *deliberate* acts of kindness, we will not win our children's affections, and the leaves will grow back as quickly as we pluck them. Love displayed to our children is the best "weed killer."

If we are consistently kind, tenderhearted, and forgiving, our affection will result in our children loving and respecting us more. They will be more inclined to obey our instructions and listen to our advice. Kind, tenderhearted, and forgiving behaviors are so powerful that if we would practice them regularly, we would experience amazing results in our families.

Be kind

Kindness may be defined as "gentleness, helpfulness, thoughtfulness, and affection toward others." Kindness may also include expressions of sympathy, compassion, and tenderness. This is not who we are naturally, but this precious attribute is needed in parenting. We must actively cultivate physical, mental, and emotional kindness toward our children. We must learn to assess *what* our children need and *when* they need it and then proceed with kindness. Kindness is the only way to reach our children at the heart level, and can turn a potentially negative confrontation into a positive learning opportunity.

Imagine this scenario: your son has just dropped a plate of food on the floor. When Mom is sponging the new carpet, it is not the time for an irritation-driven lecture on being more careful. It is the time for giving reassurance and comfort and for calmly teaching cleanup techniques. Gentle instruction is what your son needs at that moment. We do not need to make matters worse with our harsh or condemning words.

Later, when everything is in order and emotions are at rest, then it is the time for teaching and training, "What do you think caused you to drop your plate, Son? Were you not paying attention or being careless? How can we avoid this type of accident in the future?" So often, we are driven by impulse rather than kindness, by irritation rather than reason.

Be tenderhearted

Tenderness and sensitivity go together. As we are tender with our children when they need correction and are sensitive to how they may be feeling, we will touch their hearts and motivate them for good far more effectively than a thousand lectures could.

Tenderheartedness in action could be putting a hand on your son's shoulder and saying, "Well, that didn't work, did it, Son?" rather than blurting out an irritated "That was a dumb thing to do!" Tenderness would express sympathy. A "Sorry you're not feeling well," rather than an "If you would quit whining, you would probably feel better."

Tenderheartedness is a powerful resource in the parents' toolkit, one we would do well to use more skillfully and more often. God is tenderhearted with us, and we should seek to follow His example by praying for a more tenderhearted and sensitive disposition toward the precious children He has entrusted to our care.

Be forgiving

"[Forgive] one another, even as God in Christ forgave you" (Ephesians 4:32). God forgives us in trust and anticipation of our forgiving and asking forgiveness of others, especially those in our own family. If we have not handled a situation correctly with our children, if we have lost our temper, if we have neglected a need we should have fulfilled, it is only right to ask our children's forgiveness. What? Even from a little child? Yes! Jesus stated, "Inasmuch as you did it to one of the least of these My brethren, you did it to Me" (Matthew 25:40). Parents who see no need of asking their children to forgive their wrong acts while expecting the children to confess theirs are creating a double standard: one rule for the parents and another for the children. The children will come to see this as hypocrisy, which is the number one cause of rebellion in Christian young people.

When we say, "I'm sorry I lost my temper with you this morning. Will you forgive me?" we teach by example a powerful lesson in true humility. Because pride is one of those faults in our children's lives that we will encounter sooner or later, the habit of asking for forgiveness is one we need to establish.

Note: In some cases, today's displays of affection may produce suspicion in older children, causing testing behavior. Be tender and forgiving and move on!

Step Forward

☐ Determine today to be kind, tenderhearted, and forgiving toward your children.

☐ Specifically ask your children to forgive you for any past or present wrongs you have committed.

☐ Continue to refrain from jumping in with both feet to address yesterday's observations. Warning: this may be more difficult than you think!

Journal Questions and Answers

1. Rewrite 2 Chronicles 10:7 in your own words: "If you are kind to these people, and please them, and speak good words to them, they will be your servants forever."

_____

_____

_____

2. Who stands out in your mind as either kind, tender-hearted, or forgiving? What have they said or done that makes you view them in this light?

_____

_____

_____

_____

_____

3. When were you kind, tenderhearted, and forgiving today? What effect did it have on your children?

_____

_____

_____

_____

_____

4. Did any old habits of unkindness surface today? If so, were you quick to recognize them? Did you ask for forgiveness?

_____

_____

_____

_____

_____

♡

*Always . . . try to be a little
kinder than is necessary.
—James M. Barrie*

CHAPTER 4

Discovering Their Dreams

"He will turn the hearts of the fathers to the children,
and the hearts of the children to their fathers."
— Malachi 4:6

Have you ever been to an antique car show? You know the ones—polished chrome sparkles in the sunlight as excited owners display their pride and joy. As you pass a particularly interesting old car, you ask the owner, "What year is it?" "It's a 1925 Ford Model T Coupe," is the enthusiastic response. You and the owner become engaged in a lively conversation about his or her vintage car that fills you both with a sense of camaraderie. As you drive home at the end of the day, you agree with the rest of your family that it was fun to enter into the world of antique car owners and restorers. But have you ever thought about why car enthusiasts spend their time and money on such events? They obviously want to show off their cars, but they also enjoy others taking an interest in the things that interest them.

We all enjoy other people taking an interest in us. It is even more meaningful when someone we love or respect expresses an interest in us. What if you were displaying your antique car and Bill Gates were to show an interest in your 1931 Cadillac? Do you think it would make your day? Would you be eager to tell your friends? Of course, you would!

But how does showing antique cars relate to parenting?

All children, including yours, despite how indifferent they may appear at certain stages, have an inexpressible longing for their parents to show an interest in them. Some may not admit this desire because peer pressure tells them it is not cool to want Mom's and Dad's attention, but, deep down, they still long for us to take an interest in them. Our children want friends, and if they could articulate it, they would tell us they want friends they can trust, friends who love and care for them, friends who take time for them. It is our responsibility as parents to fulfill this need, to actively befriend our children by taking an interest in and getting involved in their interests and dreams. It should be our mission to be their best friends! This means, for example, that if your daughter likes bird-watching, you go bird-watching with her. Yes, even if you couldn't care less about sitting in the woods waiting for some rare little finch to show up. If your son likes to go sledding down the steepest hill in town when it is zero degrees Fahrenheit outside, then you don thermal underwear and join him! Like it or not, part of the job of being a parent is to participate in your children's interests.

When we express an interest in our children by becoming involved with our time and money, it touches them in a way that merely listening to their reports about the activities never could. Joining them in wholesome activities and interests they enjoy helps to develop a close bond, a connection that brings joy to them and, ultimately, respect to us. It also makes it easier for them to join us in the things we consider important, things like cleaning the windows, mowing the lawn, and washing the car!

The key here is *wholehearted* parental commitment to engage in the interests of our beloved children. If we are on a cell phone talking to our friends or otherwise disengaged from their world while we are supposed to be watching the birds or sledding down the hill, it neutralizes a large portion of the goodwill we could have fostered. Just as we know when our children ask, "Can we go now?" during a project that is important to us, so they know when our hearts are not fully engaged with them in their activities. Just as we can tell when they are committed to us, so they can know when we are engaged with them! Don't kid yourself. They know, and it affects our relationship with them.

It would be wise for us to investigate our children's interests, their desires, and their dreams. Give them opportunities to participate in making some decisions by asking them for their opinions and preferences: If you could choose where we go on vacation this year, where would it be? Or, What would you like to do if we set the next three Sunday afternoons aside for some special family activities? When we understand our children's desires, we are more prepared to meet their needs.

It is a sad fact that some parents are too self-centered to take this kind of genuine interest in their children. They would rather play golf with their buddies or shop with their friends than be with their children. If we repeatedly miss opportunities to spend quality time with our children while we live under the same roof, we unthinkingly prepare the way for them to be more emotionally distant from us in the future. Taking the time now to create special memories together will go far in preserving family unity in the years ahead. Our scripture for today declares the order of events: first, we must turn our hearts toward our children, and then they will turn their hearts to us.

Step Forward

☐ In a natural way, search out the interests and dreams of each of your children. Make sure your questioning does not come across as interrogation! Spread this activity out over the whole day.

☐ Talk with your spouse and make some initial plans to engage in your children's wholesome interests and dreams. In the chapters ahead, specifically chapters 7, 8, 10, and 14, you will have opportunities to put these plans into action.

☐ Continue tuning in to your children's world by being observant. Their rooms could also hold clues to their interests or dreams.

☐ Continue to pray specifically for each of your children.

Journal Questions and Answers

1. Rewrite Malachi 4:6 in your own words: "He will turn the hearts of the fathers to the children, and the hearts of the children to their fathers."

_____

_____

_____

_____

_____

_____

2. What interests do your children have? List each child and his or her interests.

_____

_____

_____

_____

_____

_____

_____

3. What dreams do your children have? List each child and his or her dreams. (For example, an interest could be astronomy; the corresponding dream would be to have his or her own telescope.)

_____

_____

_____

_____

_____

_____

_____

_____

4. What plans do you have to participate in your children's interests and dreams?

_____

_____

_____

_____

_____

_____

_____

_____

A child seldom needs a good talking
to as a good listening to.
— Robert Brault

CHAPTER 5

Review and Revisit
Chapters 1-4

*"Be strong and do not let your hands be weak,
for your work shall be rewarded!"*
—*2 Chronicles 15:7*

Imagine your teenage child has an important math test in the morning. Your inquiry as to whether he has prepared for the test is met with a casual, "Well, we have covered it all in class already. I should be OK."

I am sure most of us would prefer that our child would spend a little time going over his previous work, refreshing his memory on the topics covered. Such a review is the purpose of this chapter. It provides an opportunity to finish exercises that were not completed and to revisit those areas that could use some extra time, thoughts, or actions. Because we have done something once does not mean we have done it sufficiently to ensure success. Anything worth doing will demand effort on our part, and the well-being and spiritual growth of our children deserves our best and most thorough effort!

Chapter 1, "What We Need to Succeed"

Are you still feeling enthusiastic about investing time in your family? It's a good sign if it seems that reading this book and completing each chapter's assignments are crowding out other things that need to be done. Those other things would wait if you were in the hospital! So doesn't it stand to reason that these things can wait while you give your children the time needed to bind their hearts to yours for now and eternity? If you don't have the time now, when will you?

Chapter 1 helped us lay the foundations for success by praying for God's power, for determination, and for commitment. This is a prayer we need to keep before the Lord, especially if we sense our determination is waning. Feelings of failure will also undermine our commitment and determination. But remember, anything in life worth having is going to take special effort. Prayer is the key to opening Heaven's resources. Continue to pray for power, determination, and commitment.

Chapter 2, "What in Their World Is Going On?"

The focus of chapter 2—observing our children with the intention of gaining a deeper understanding of them—likely resulted in discoveries that caused us some concern. In this case, ignorance is not bliss. We need to know what is going on in our children's world. That you actually made discoveries should be regarded as a positive step. If you didn't learn anything new while doing the assignments suggested in chapter 2, take the time to explore your children's bedrooms again. If *JPEG images*, *social networking,* or *text messaging* are foreign terms to you, go online and find out what they are. The Web site www.internetsafety101.org is a good place to begin. If you do not have access to a computer or the Internet, or if you are not familiar with operating a computer, ask someone you trust who is computer savvy for assistance. Being ignorant of what your children are doing on the Internet will work against you, possibly even undermining much of your effort in other areas.

Chapter 3, "The Results of Affection"

This chapter focused on the need to treat your children

with kindness, tenderheartedness, and forgiveness, and was potentially the most important lesson so far. If you can re-visit only one chapter, chapter 3 is the one to choose. The combined effect of practicing these three behaviors will smooth the way for opening communication and dissolving hard feelings that may have accumulated in your children's hearts. In human interaction, it is obvious that our behavior influences others. As our children observe us being kind, ten-derhearted, and forgiving toward them, we make it easier for them to reflect these traits back to us. A hug can have a sig-nificant effect! We have the ability to be the most important influence in our children's lives. Let's take advantage of this opportunity!

Chapter 4, "Discovering Their Dreams"

Identifying our children's interests and dreams and starting to develop a plan to fulfill them was the theme of the previous chapter. What a joy to take an active role in making our children happier! Keep your plans before God in prayer; share them with your spouse or a friend as ap-propriate.

Step Forward

☐ Look over the Step Forward sections of chapters 1–4. Review or revisit those activities you realize could use more attention.

☐ Read your journal entries for chapters 1–4 again, adding to them as necessary.

☐ Spend some time with your spouse comparing notes, observations, and ideas. If you are not united, seek to listen carefully to the other's perspective. Pray together for unity in guiding your children.

Journal Questions and Answers

1. Rewrite 2 Chronicles 15:7 in your own words: "Be strong and do not let your hands be weak, for your work shall be rewarded!"

_____
_____
_____
_____
_____

2. What areas did you review or revisit? Why?

_____
_____
_____
_____
_____

3. What did you and your spouse discuss today as you compared notes, observations, and ideas? Make a journal entry responding to your spouse's or discussion partner's thoughts.

_____
_____
_____
_____
_____

♡

*The eye's a better pupil
and more willing than the ear.
—Edgar A. Guest*

CHAPTER 6

A Most Powerful Motivator

A word fitly spoken is like apples of gold in pictures of silver.
—Proverbs 25:11, KJV

"I didn't mean to, Mom. Honestly, I didn't! It was my friend from school. He kept daring me to do it and so—well, I just did it." We can probably all relate to this childhood experience of doing something even though it was not in our hearts to do it. Maybe we gave in to peer pressure or followed the crowd, but we have all done things that we would not have done but for the encouragement of others.

This is why big businesses spend millions of dollars every year on advertising. It works! Through the influence and encouragement of commercials, magazine ads, and billboards, consumers buy things they would otherwise have done without. Again we see that consistent encouragement is very effective!

Given this fact, it is a wonder we use encouragement so infrequently to inspire right choices in our children. Unfortunately, many parents have underestimated and ignored the most powerful of motivators—encouraging words! Scripture states this truth with a memorable image: "A word fitly spoken is like apples of gold in settings of silver" (Proverbs 25:11).

How effectively do we encourage our children? Every honest parent will admit there is room for improvement.

Let's look at the main reasons we do not use encouraging words as often as we should and also look at the results of implementing this powerful motivator for good.

Reason 1

We often neglect to use encouraging words because our natural tendency is to focus on addressing the present problem.

An example. A mother assigns a child the task of cleaning his bedroom. Later in the day, she strolls in to check his progress. She notices books on the floor, a muddy soccer ball on the shelf, and a dirty sock peeking out from under the bed. With a hint of frustration in her voice, she addresses the problem as she sees it. "You missed some things. Those books need to be put away, and what is that filthy ball doing on the bookshelf?" Glancing down at the stray sock, she asks, "Why didn't you clean under your bed?" Can you relate to her method of response?

The solution. What was the outcome of this all-to-common scenario? Eventually, the mother got a clean room, but she missed the opportunity to encourage her child in the work he had done and to foster a desire to keep his bedroom neat in the future.

The mother's first reaction was to point out what the child had missed. In reality, it was the parent who missed something! This parent, like so many of us, was focused only on fixing the present problems, namely, the books on the floor, the dirty ball on the shelf, and the dirty sock under the bed! This parent could have used encouragement to motivate her child. "I see you have been busy. Your room looks much better! You did a good job making your bed, and I see most of your clothes have been put away. You even vacuumed! Well done! Now wouldn't it be nice if your room looked this neat all of the time? If we put those books on the shelf, take the ball out to the garage, and put that sock in the hamper, it will be perfect!" Do you see the difference? Can you understand how the child would be encouraged to make more of an effort to keep his room clean? The first approach yields a tidy home; the second approach yields a happy home.

Reason 2

We often fail to encourage because we do not look at life through our children's eyes.

An example. As busy presenters at a seminar series, we had little quality time with our children throughout the day. Back in our room one evening, we asked our six-year-old son, "How was today for you, Caleb?" His eyes immediately filled, and through the tears, he said, "I didn't get any popcorn." We had heard the announcement that free popcorn would be available that evening, but, because we had other commitments, we paid little attention. We missed an opportunity to affirm our son, who had sat patiently through all the meetings, because we did not see life through his six-year-old viewpoint!

The solution. We need to become more sensitive to how our children relate to the various situations that make up their world. They have their disappointments just as we have ours. Obviously, parents are not affected if they miss out on free popcorn, but to our son, missing this treat was comparable to our missing an opportunity to get 75 percent off on a vacation package. We would be disappointed too!

If during that busy day we had occasionally looked at life though our son's eyes, we would have instantly recognized the value of the popcorn opportunity. We regretted missing our chance to encourage and reward him for his good behavior throughout the day. Parenting is a learning experience!

Reason 3

We often don't consider using encouraging words because the child is simply behaving the way he or she is "supposed" to.

An example. As you walk into the library with your little children, you tell them, "Please stay close to Mommy, and remember, we have to be very quiet in here." As you peruse shelf after shelf, looking for the right book, your children obediently stand quietly by your side.

The solution. While no solution is needed here, we must learn to see that every good choice our children make provides us with a golden opportunity to give encouragement. In this situation, encouragement could be given by simply saying, "Thank you for staying near me and being so quiet at the library. I appreciated it." An appreciative hug would reinforce the good choices our children have made. Encouragement for right doing strengthens our child's desire to make more good choices in the future.

A word of caution here. We need to be careful to encourage rather than flatter. Saying, "You were the best-behaved children in the whole library," would be unwise flattery rather than encouragement. Flattery appeals to pride and could be detrimental to our children over time.

Step Forward

☐ Talk with the Lord today about becoming a more encouraging parent. Specifically ask Him to remind you to be encouraging when an opportunity presents itself.

☐ Look for at least three ways to actively encourage each of your children today.

☐ Show physical affection to your children today. Give them a hug or a kiss, tousle their hair, whatever is appropriate.

Journal Questions and Answers

1. Rewrite Proverbs 25:11 in your own words: "A word fitly spoken is like apples of gold in settings of silver."

Write it in the first person, that is, "My words . . . ," or "When I . . ."

_____

_____

_____

_____

_____

_____

2. How did your children respond to the encouragement you gave them today?

_____

_____

_____

_____

_____

_____

3. Think back over the past few years. Who has encouraged you to make better choices, and how did they do it?

_____

_____

_____

_____

_____

_____

A word of encouragement makes
a world of difference.

CHAPTER 7

One-on-One
Part 1

Then He took them [the disciples] and went aside privately
into a deserted place.
—Luke 9:10

Various social situations create different dynamics among the participants. When we get together in a group social setting with no particular purpose other than to have an enjoyable time, the atmosphere tends to be light. But one of the beauties of one-on-one time with a spouse, child, or friend is that our time together tends to be more serious, more intimate, and more unifying. It can be a profitable and gratifying experience for both parties.

How long has it been since you experienced quality one-on-one time with your children? In this busy world, we must schedule individual time with our children if we are to have a close heart connection with them. This time together doesn't have to involve entertainment or excitement; it needs only to be in an environment where we can enjoy some special time one on one. It could be fixing our child's bicycle in the shop, taking a drive together, or even just washing the car. We should not expect to spend the whole day in heart-to-heart conversation with our child. That may be possible in the future, but it is not likely to be our experience the first time.

An activity my children and I [Paul] especially enjoy is downhill skiing. "Thrifty Thursday," as it is called at our nearby ski resort, often finds us hitting the slopes together. While our communication is mostly limited to "follow me" or "watch out!" as we make our way down the hill, it is on the chairlift that we find time to talk. As well as reliving the previous run and planning the next one, I often use this opportunity to ask questions. "So, what's happening in school these days, Hannah?" "Hey, Caleb, I notice that you are enjoying that book about the Wright Brothers. What are you learning?" Asking these types of questions is simply a way of opening up conversation between parent and child. I have no real agenda during these interactions. I just want them to feel free to talk to their hearts' content. My part is to listen.

I [Carolyn] find taking one of my children to town with me, maybe for a doctor's appointment or to buy shoes, is a great opportunity for that special one-on-one time. There is plenty of opportunity during our hour-long drive to town to ask those questions that reveal what is happening in their hearts. On one particular day in town, as Hannah and I were paying for our meal at our favorite salad bar, the cashier commented on our mother-daughter date. There were tears in her eyes as she explained how she had longed for a daughter of her own and that she was very encouraged to see us spending time together. The conversation made our one-on-one time all the more significant that day.

Jesus loved the crowd, but He also had a faithful regard for the one-person audience. He recognized the value of one-on-one time with the precious individuals He sought to save. Christ also longed for time alone with His disciples in order to instruct them specifically. Luke 9:10 tells us, "He took them [the disciples] and went aside privately into a deserted place." Likewise, we need to learn the importance of one-on-one time, realizing it can be a special time and an important building block in the relationship between parent and child.

Obviously, children vary in preferences and personality. We will need to thoughtfully choose activities that will interest a particular child. We encourage you to keep your planned activities simple and natural. We could take our children to the movies, a theme park, or a ball game, but these types of activities could work against the purpose of the time together. Be careful that the activities you choose are tools that promote conversation, and are not communication stoppers. It is not easy to have quality conversation in a dark theater while watching a loud movie!

Below are some suggestions of activities you could do for one-on-one time with your children.

- Take your child out to eat, letting them choose the restaurant.
- Plan to stay home when everyone else is out and do a puzzle together.
- Take your child to a special place to bike, hike, skate, or ski.
- Go for a walk.
- If you have little children, take a walk in a park and feed ducks.
- Go to a zoo, a museum, or a science center.

Review chapter 4, "Discovering Their Dreams," for more ideas.

One-on-one time is not always easy to arrange, but as we take time to *do* something we haven't done before, we open up the way for *progress* we haven't seen before.

Step Forward

☐ Give some thought and prayer to how you can spend quality one-on-one time with one of your children today. If it is impractical to do it today, make definite plans to do something in the next few days. Remember Ecclesiastes 9:10, the scripture of chapter 1, "Whatever your hand finds to do, do it with your might." This is a step that is too important to overlook!

☐ Before spending time together, think of a few simple questions you would like to ask your child to stimulate conversation. Avoid questions that can be answered with a short Yes or No.

Note: Once we have committed to this special one-on-one time, we need to keep our word! To break the appointment once it has been made sends a damaging message to the child. In chapter 14, we will have an opportunity for one-on-one time with another child.

Journal Questions and Answers

1 Luke 9:10 says, "Then He took them [the disciples] and went aside privately into a deserted place." Why do you think Jesus did that? What are some of the disadvantages of leading busy lives?

_____

_____

_____

_____

_____

_____

_____

_____

_____

_____

_____

_____

2. What are you planning today for one-on-one time with one of your children?

_____

_____

_____

_____

_____

_____

3. How was your one-on-one time? What did you talk about? Who did most of the talking?

_____

_____

_____

_____

_____

_____

4. What, if anything, would you do differently next time?

_____

_____

_____

_____

_____

_____

_____

In communication,
listen carefully to the unspoken.

CHAPTER 8

But It's Not My Birthday!

"If you then, being evil, know how to give good gifts to your children, how much more will your Father who is in heaven give good things to those who ask Him!"
— *Matthew 7:11*

Children become excited as their birthdays approach, not so much because they mark another year of blessings, but because they look forward to gifts, cards, and special times with family and friends. While more conscious of the blessings received, parents look forward to the opportunities to express their love to their children. As selfish as humanity has become, we still love to give special gifts to our children, even if they have given us a few more gray hairs in the past year!

Today's scripture characterizes this parental love and states an important truth. "If you then, being evil, know how to give good gifts to your children, how much more will your Father who is in heaven give good things to those who ask Him!" (Matthew 7:11). Contemplate this question for a moment. How much more willing is God to give good things to us than we are to give good things to our children? It's a question we cannot answer; we simply are invited to ponder God's generosity. Our response can only be, we are sinners; He is an Infinite God. We live in a corrupt world; He dwells in heaven's glory. We have limited time and money; God's resources are limitless! We parents have a God who is much more willing to give to us than we are to give to our children. The gifts of God are priceless; mere money, even millions of dollars, could never secure them.

Today's chapter focuses on our need for one of these gifts. Today, our love for our children needs to be more than human love, more than parental love. It needs to be God's love working through us. For this divine love to become a reality in us, our human selfishness, excuses, and false reasoning have to be put away. We can learn a valuable lesson as we contemplate the price God was willing to pay to capture our attention and draw us to Him.

Heaven's love is more than desire, more than emotion, and more than future plans. God's love is expressed in *action*. God the Son stepped down from the throne of the universe, emptied Himself of everything but love, and came to this dark world to die for us. He had desire, He had emotion, and He had distant plans, but they all culminated in an action that touched humanity. Without the action of leaving heaven, coming to this earth to live and walk with us, there would be no Christmas story, no miracles, no Calvary, and no glorious Resurrection morning! It is not just the thought that counts; the thought needs to be lived out and made tangible!

Picture yourself stranded on the roadside with your vehicle out of gas. When you call your friends, they express a desire to help and express how bad they feel about your situation, but they tell you they are unable to come right away. However, you need more than a sympathetic voice on the phone if you are going to make it to the airport in time. Next, you dial your parents' number. Dad answers. You haven't even finished explaining your predicament when Dad says, "I'll be there in ten minutes." Which response touches your heart and fills you with relief? It was true two thousand years ago when Christ was born in Bethlehem, and it still rings true today—actions speak louder than words!

In chapter 4, we were challenged with discovering our children's dreams and making plans to participate in them. Today is the day we begin to make their dreams come true. This exercise is a vital part of drawing our children closer to us and, ultimately, closer to the Lord. Take a moment to review chapter 4, along with your journal entries.

Parents, I know we have things to do and places to go; but *today* is the day we make concrete plans to help our children turn meaningful dreams into a reality. We can begin to fulfill dreams that will enrich their lives in some way—this is more than just another gift.

In some cases, it may not be possible to make their dreams a reality right now. There may not be time to drive the two hundred miles to pick up that musical instrument they have been wanting or to go on a special trip. In that case, today is the day we make an announcement. Using your God-given creativity, think of an exciting way to share your intentions. Maybe a treasure hunt around the home that leads to a card explaining your plans. Maybe a special family meal followed by an announcement of your plans to help your children fulfill their dreams.

Collaborate and calculate before you commit. Where possible, brainstorm with your spouse and make plans together. Count the cost before you make any promises. While your heart may be stirred in the moment to make some grand plans, be certain you can follow through. God understands your budget, and He can bless as you work within it. It is not always the most elaborate plan or the most expensive option that will make a lasting impression. Be sure you are fulfilling your children's dreams and not your own. This is a precious opportunity to be used intelligently, and it is better to aim for a reachable goal than to be unrealistic and miss it altogether.

A friend of ours recently shared a memory with us. "When my dad came home one evening with a brand-new softball, it was an it's-not-my-birthday moment. We were poor, but my dad decided he could afford a new softball. It was only a small thing, but it made a big impression on me, one I still remember today."

As we allow God to work through us today, to touch the hearts of our children in a meaningful way, we are becoming an active part of Heaven's plan to save our children. We are indeed being God's fellow workers (see 1 Corinthians 3:9). What a joy, what a privilege!

Step Forward

☐ Pray specifically for God to give you *His* love for your children.

☐ As appropriate, collaborate and determine what your plans for your children will involve and how you will announce it.

☐ Carry out your plans to fulfill their dreams today or in the next few days.

Journal Questions and Answers

1. Rewrite Matthew 7:11 in your own words: "If you then, being evil, know how to give good gifts to your children, how much more will your Father who is in heaven give good things to those who ask Him!"

_____

_____

_____

_____

_____

_____

_____

_____

_____

2. What did you do to fulfill your children's dreams? Be detailed.

_____

_____

_____

_____

_____

_____

_____

_____

_____

3. How do you think making your children's dreams a reality has or will affect their relationship with you?

_____

_____

_____

_____

_____

_____

_____

_____

_____

You can give without loving, but you can never love without giving.
—Author Unknown

53

CHAPTER 9

Review and Revisit
Chapters 6-8

*Let us not grow weary while doing good, for in due season
we shall reap if we do not lose heart.*
—Galatians 6:9

The road to success is lined with turnouts containing idling vehicles. If the previous chapter went well, then today you may be tempted to take a break in a rest area, for the high of success can sometimes be followed by a low. The Old Testament hero Elijah, after standing alone against eight hundred fifty ungodly priests and gaining one of the most inspiring victories of all time, found himself the next day in such fear of a vengeful queen that he asked God to let him die. While we may not be that discouraged, let's not entertain any thoughts of giving up our efforts to win our children's hearts. We have covered much ground in completing these first eight chapters and are making precious progress! We may not have done everything right, but as we remind ourselves of where we started, we should be encouraged. We began by praying for power, commitment, and determination before turning our efforts to tune in to our children's world. We started focusing on giving affection and discovering their dreams. In the past few chapters, we have rediscovered the value of encouraging words, spent some long overdue one-on-one time with our children, and participated in making dreams come true. What a beautiful promise today's text is when we really believe it: "Let us not grow weary while doing good, for in due season we shall reap if we do not lose heart" (Galatians 6:9). Let's keep pressing on. Now is not the time to lose heart!

Chapter 6, "A Most Powerful Motivator"

Here we outlined the power of encouragement as a tool to win our children's hearts. We noted how the advertising industry successfully uses encouraging words in commercials to motivate us to purchase products and how peer pressure sometimes persuades us do things we wouldn't normally do.

The beauty of encouragement in the family is that not only are the children blessed, but the parents are too. Just as we feel horrible after we vent impatient words, we feel a sense of satisfaction when we encourage. Affirming words bring sunshine into the home and promote a positive atmosphere that all will enjoy.

Where our family lives, we see temperatures fall and lakes freeze in the winter. Rather than becoming hermits by the woodstove, we seize the opportunity for some outdoor fun and head down to our pond with ice skates in hand. Ice is slippery to begin with, but add narrow blades to your boots and you really have a wild combination! While trying to stay upright myself, I [Paul] had the task of introducing our two little children to the joys of skating. They would fall, and so would I, but we would get back up and try again. I had no words of wisdom to give my children and could demonstrate no helpful techniques to make learning to skate any easier. The only tool I had was encouragement. Each time they fell I would give them a little pep talk and encourage them to try again. Little by little, we all made progress; and although we still have room for improvement, we can now play hockey together! As with skating, so it is with life. Encouragement picks up our spirits and helps us to continue trying when things are hard. This truth has carried down through the ages.

"A word fitly spoken is like apples of gold in settings of silver" (Proverbs 25:11).

Chapter 7, "One-on-One, Part 1"

Chapter 7 called us to spend one-on-one time with our children. We were encouraged to have some questions prepared to stimulate conversation and either to watch for or make an opportunity to present them. One-on-one time is more personal than group conversation; it feels safe. It is a time when children feel freer to share their hearts, their fears, their hopes, and their dreams.

If we have not had much individual time with our children, we may be surprised how little we know of their lives. Do we know their hurts, their disappointments, their joys, and their hopes? If our daughter is to be free to tell us about her feelings for a young man in the future, the path of communication must be well-trodden beforehand. The future is not the time to say, "We need to talk!" Now is the time to learn to talk to each other. As we take advantage of opportunities to spend quality time talking with our children, it will become more natural for them and our conversations will become less awkward. Give them time to develop their communication skills. Perhaps up to this point, most of our conversations with our children have been shallow. They will need time to become accustomed to more heartfelt communication. Gradually, they will become more and more comfortable with deeper conversation. Step-by-step, our relationship will be nurtured, our influence will be enlarged, and our love for each other will be strengthened.

Chapter 8, "But It's Not My Birthday!"

This chapter challenged us to give something special to our children and, in some way, make one of their dreams come true. Just as when someone does something special for us, it endears our hearts to them, so when we go out of our way to bless our children, their hearts will be drawn to us. It takes more than good intentions to give the fullest blessing—it takes action.

If you were unable to fulfill a dream as discussed in chapter 8, use today to plan or accomplish this important step. Our efforts will be repaid many times over as we draw closer to our children. Let's show our thankfulness for them by fulfilling an important dream in a meaningful way. The joy of accomplishment awaits us!

Step Forward

☐ If your conscience is reminding you of an area you did not complete or that you need to review, be sure to follow through. This could be the Lord's prompting!

☐ Take some time with your spouse (or friend if you are a single parent) and compare notes and experiences. Keep your conversation positive and solution oriented. Have special prayer time together, committing yourself afresh to complete this twenty-six-step plan with your children.

Journal Questions and Answers

1. Rewrite Galatians 6:9 in your own words and in the first person: "Let us not grow weary while doing good, for in due season we shall reap if we do not lose heart."

_____

_____

_____

_____

_____

_____

_____

2. What areas did you review and revisit, and what were the results?

_____

_____

_____

_____

_____

_____

_____

_____

_____

3. Write out your commitment to complete this entire twenty-six-step plan. Sign and date it.

_____

_____

_____

_____

_____

_____

_____

_____

_____

Our heavenly Father has a thousand ways to provide for us, of which we know nothing.
—Ellen G. White

CHAPTER 10

Invest in the Best

*Behold, how good and how pleasant it is for brethren
to dwell together in unity!*
—Psalm 133:1

"It's quick, it's easy, and guaranteed to save you time"; I'm sure you have seen such ads. But in reality, even with the multitude of time-saving devices available today, we have less free time than previous generations had. Studies have shown that families spend 40 percent less time together today than they did a generation ago. Why is that? It is because the enemy of God and man, the devil and his helpers, are on a campaign to fill up our schedules. Their motto could well be, Promise them time, but steal it from them; tell them it's simple, but make it complicated. If you have ever tried to pair up Bluetooth devices or program your oven to delay the baking cycle, you know what we are talking about. Human beings are seemingly trapped on the treadmill of life, and it's moving faster with each passing year. But full schedules are only half the story.

Another thief of family time is the lure of technology that distracts us from our priorities. Technology is consuming our time, our energy, and, ultimately, our happiness. With our lips, we say our children are everything to us, but our actions do not support our words. We spend more time talking on the phone or browsing the Internet than we do with our own flesh and blood. As a result, our children learn to live in their own world, and thus, the groundwork is laid for the next generation to spend even less time together. The good news is that today's chapter is designed to change our awareness and put us on the path toward making our family the priorities that we long for them to be!

Today, we introduce "family time," a special portion of each day during which all members of the family leave behind their school assignments, their work, and their entertainments to spend time together. It may seem impossible to squeeze one more thing into your already hectic schedule, but it can be done! Families have done it in times past, and we personally know of many families, including our own, who enjoy family time today.

Let's look at one scenario of how to introduce family time into your home. Before Dad leaves for work, he calls the family together. He announces in his most authoritative voice that everyone needs to be in the living room that evening immediately after dinner. No matter how many times the children ask why or beg for more information, they are told that they will find out after dinner. The mystery is part of the intrigue. That evening, when the family is assembled, you present your plan to implement family time. Place this new concept in a positive light, as a time to do fun things together. Ask your children what they would like to do during this time, and don't rule anything out at this point. Next, allocate an evening to each child and parent for which they will be responsible for choosing the activity.

Ideas for family-time activities

Ideas for family-time activities can include the following:

- Play Frisbee or ball at home or at local park.
- Do a puzzle together.
- Try out a new recipe.
- Repair something.

- Participate in a sponsored walk, ride, or swim.
- Go on a bike ride.
- Start a family project: crafts, mechanics, Legos, and so on.
- Jump on a trampoline.
- Play indoor or outdoor hide-and-seek.
- Clean a car, yours or the neighbor's (ask first).
- Go to a park and feed the ducks.
- Teach your pet a new trick.
- Play hide the thimble/quarter.
- Go out to eat.
- Eat at home and let the children make the meal.
- Organize your family photos.
- Watch old home videos of your family.
- Read a book.
- Rearrange the furniture.
- Give the dog a bath.
- Clean up the yard
- Weed the garden or flower beds.
- Call a family friend on a phone with a speaker feature.
- Go shopping as a family.
- Go skating or Rollerblading.
- Visit a neighbor who lives alone.
- Make a surprise visit to your extended family.
- Go swimming.
- Fly a kite.
- Plan a vacation.
- Any wholesome activity you enjoyed as a child.

General guidelines for effective family times

Here are some general guidelines for effective family times:

- Schedule your family time. It does not have to be every evening, but make a plan and stick with it.
- Make a family time calendar and post it so everyone knows what is planned.

- As far as possible, involve the entire family in the same general activity. If two groups develop, Mom should be in one group and Dad in the other.
- Prohibit answering the phone or checking text messages or e-mail during family time.
- Seek a healthy balance in the activities rather than being all fun or all work. Allowing each person to choose the activity on his or her assigned evening helps to keep this balance.
- Plan ahead for those activities that are a bit more involved.

The benefits of regular family time are many. Engaging in a wholesome activity strengthens friendships, minimizes little annoyances, generates enthusiasm, and draws hearts closer. Family time has the effect of uniting a family and making today's scripture more of a reality. "Behold, how good and how pleasant it is for brethren [family] to dwell together in unity!" (Psalm 133:1).

Step Forward

☐ Continue praying for your family, particularly that schedules (parents' included) can be adjusted so that you can spend more time together.

☐ Make a list of at least ten activities you think your entire family would enjoy.

☐ As the leaders of your family, institute some version of family time today.

Journal Questions and Answers

1. What challenges do you anticipate in implementing family time, and how can they be overcome?

_____
_____
_____
_____
_____
_____

2. What time-saving devices or activities have been stealing you away from your children? What are you going to do to change that?

_____
_____
_____
_____
_____
_____

3. How and when do you plan to institute family time?

_____
_____
_____
_____
_____
_____

The work never goes away,
but the children will.

CHAPTER 11

Learning Their Limits

*"My grace is sufficient for you,
for My strength is made perfect in weakness."*
—2 Corinthians 12:9

As the minibus came to a halt, the driver announced, "Boys, this is where you get out. Collect your bags and run to the house. It's about two-thirds of a mile down that gravel driveway. The last one there takes out the trash for a week." This was my initiation to a three-week character-building course sponsored by my employer.

Once we had recovered from running with our suitcases, we unpacked and assembled in the courtyard for our next instructions. Pointing at a two-hundred-foot grassy embankment, the instructor said, "This is Punishment Hill. I will be timing you as you run to the top and back down. Be sure to go as quickly as you can." About fifteen minutes later, we are all back at the bottom of the hill, huffing and puffing from the exertion. "Now listen, boys, if you disobey any orders, for any reason, you will be sent up Punishment Hill. Each time you must better your previous time. Do you understand?"

"Yes, sir!" was our unanimous reply! We were beginning to get the picture. There wasn't going to be any goofing off on this course!

It was about five days later when a number of us failed a room inspection. "All four of you meet me at the bottom of

Punishment Hill in three minutes," was the command. "Remember, you have to beat your previous time. Are you ready? Three, two, one, go!" Up and down we went, just as fast as our seventeen-year-old legs would take us. Three of us beat our previous record, but the other boy was a few seconds short. "You have five minutes to catch your breath; then you're off again," he was told. His second attempt also failed. We wondered what would happen now. The officer said in an unwavering, yet somehow encouraging voice, "You have five minutes to catch your breath, young man, and then you're off again. You can do it!" The unspoken question went through everyone's mind, How could he run that hill again and better his time when he was so tired? But off he went again, pounding his way up the steep hillside. On his way down, we cheered and shouted, "You can do it! Keep going!" To everyone's relief, he beat his record.

I learned a valuable lesson that day, one I have never forgotten. We are capable of more than we think we are. Indeed, 2 Corinthians 12:9 is so true, "My grace is sufficient for you, for My strength is made perfect in weakness." In all areas of life, when the expectations are higher, the standard is elevated, and more grace and determination are called into action. Goals we thought unattainable come within our grasp. This is a valuable lesson for parents. So often we have low expectations for our children, but they are capable of much more than we think they are. With careful instruction from Mom, a three- to four-year-old can load the dishwasher, set the table, or hang up his or her clothes. A five- to six-year-old can help locate items in the grocery store or make a simple sandwich. A seven- to nine-year-old can safely learn to cook, clean the bathroom, or use a drill. By the age of ten to twelve, if well-trained and encouraged, a child should be capable of almost any task around the home, given he or she has the physical strength to do it.

By giving our children these responsibilities, they experience the joy of usefulness and the delight of accomplishment, something video games and cartoons can never give them. Parents are rewarded too. Our daughter cooked her first "all on her own" dinner when she was ten years old. I can still hardly believe our son, at the age of six and a half, walked all but one mile of a thirteen-mile hike in Glacier National Park. True, it was a long way for his little legs—and ours, for that matter. But the point remains; he did it. He was exhausted but elated and still had enough energy to play around the campsite that evening.

This being said, we need to recognize that different children excel in different areas. We must not expect the same abilities of all. What one finds easy, another may find difficult, even within the same family. These variations occur in many areas—gross motor skills, fine motor skills, and language skills. But all should be taught useful life skills such as cooking, cleaning, gardening, and care of clothing and motor vehicles.

How can we encourage our children to reach their fullest potential when they don't believe they can? One of the most effective ways is by example. As Edgar A. Guest said, "The eye's a better pupil and more willing than the ear." If our children see us attempting and conquering hard things, it will influence them in ways words never could. The wise man said, "Train up a child in the way he should go" (Proverbs 22:6). He did not say, "Tell a child." Training involves instruction, demonstration, correction, and repetition.

One trap we must avoid is expecting our children to press through their difficulties while we make no effort to press through ours. It is unfair for siblings to be told not to yell at each other when they have witnessed their parents being involved in a shouting match just a few days earlier. The old saying "Do as I say, not as I do" is not good motivation.

Finally, be prayerful in your expectations; they have power for good or evil. If we expect too much of our children, we will not only steal from them the joy of victory but will set ourselves up for frustration and disappointment. Too high of an expectation is as much to be avoided as too low. If in doubt, take counsel from the Old Testament patriarch Jacob who, when moving his family a long distance on foot, determined to "lead on softly" (Genesis 33:14, KJV).

Step Forward

☐ Pray specifically about the expectations you have for your children. Determine if your expectations need to be adjusted.

☐ If you are presently holding either your spouse or children to unreasonable expectations, release those expectations today.

☐ Look for one way to raise a standard in your home, not solely by instruction, but by example as well.

Journal Questions and Answers

1. Rewrite 2 Corinthians 12:9 in your own words and in the first person: "My grace is sufficient for you, for My strength is made perfect in weakness."

_____

_____

_____

_____

_____

_____

_____

_____

2. For each of your children, write out any changes you would like to make in your expectations of them.

_____

_____

_____

_____

_____

_____

_____

_____

_____

3. What did you do to raise a standard today? Was there any response from family members?

_____

_____

_____

_____

_____

_____

_____

_____

_____

♡

A man's children and his garden
both reflect the amount of weeding done
during the growing season.
—Author Unknown

CHAPTER 12

A Secret Life

God will bring every work into judgment,
including every secret thing, whether good or evil.
—Ecclesiastes 12:14

Training our children and growing a garden have many similarities. Gardeners desire a bumper crop; parents long to see the fruits of helpfulness, courtesy, and respect in their children. Experienced gardeners have learned the value of recognizing cause and effect. If the leaves of tomato plants are wilting, the plants need water. That's an easy one. What if the leaves have a purple tinge? A little research would reveal the plants need more phosphorus. With the essential element added to the soil, the plant begins to thrive and eventually bears fruit.

Parenting, however, includes many more variables than gardening does. How are parents to know whether a purple stage (hair or fingernails) is normal? They do not have a guidebook telling them just exactly how a healthy eight-year-old should look and behave. Each child is unique.

Yet parents have a major advantage over gardeners. We can talk to our children! Yes, some people talk to their plants, but, unlike plants, our children can answer questions. They can tell us what they are thinking and feeling and what they need! You probably remember, as we do, those sleepless nights when your baby would cry for what seemed like hours. Oh, how we wished we could just ask him or her what was wrong. But now that he or she is older and cries out in different ways, we don't always think to ask those important questions. However, we do not have to guess or look in a book to find out why our child's hair now has a tinge of purple; we can ask them! But before we will receive the answers we need, we first need to learn the right approach and the right questions to ask.

An irritated approach

"When you were out who knows where, I found this letter, young lady. Don't you know this boy is a good-for-nothing waste of space?" Tearing up the letter and enclosed photo, the parent declares, "You will have nothing more to do with him, do you understand me?" Did this parent get his or her point across? Oh, yes. But how well was it received, how effective will the confrontation be in the long term, and did the parent communicate his or her real concern? If the inappropriate relationship continues, it will likely go underground and grow there.

A tactful approach

"Susie, we need to talk. We found this letter the other day. Is there anything you would like to tell us about it?" Give Susie time to answer and let her verbalize all of her thoughts. Your "plant" is talking to you! Then ask another question, "What do you know about this young man's past? Has he dated other girls?"

The key to productive communication with our children and youth is to first understand their thoughts. Let them talk while you listen with a heart to *really* understand where they are coming from. We all think differently. Ask questions that investigate, such as, What do you know about his past? rather than making absolute statements, such as You will have nothing more to do with him. Listen to your child's thoughts and then try to lead him or her to see the bigger picture, a more mature view of the situation. Bring in aspects or implications he or she may not have thought about, not as your trump card to clinch the case but as a legitimate attempt to help him or her analyze the situation. Try not to get hung up on nonessentials or tangent issues but keep the conversation on the subject at hand. Most of all, be sensitive to the still, small Voice of the Holy Spirit. Intensity, passion, and volume will not help. Remember, we are seeking to win the heart, not the argument.

Upon suspecting a problem is developing with one of their children, some parents—perhaps to avoid confrontation or perhaps they are unsure of what to do—ignore the situation, hoping it will resolve itself. They see evidence of a problem but cannot bring themselves to deal with it. As time passes, the situation develops, often to the point that they are forced to become involved. Unfortunately, ignoring the problem will not make it go away! Ignoring the purple leaves will not help the plant to thrive. We may not want to deal with the situation, but it is part of our job as parents. Usually, it is wise to intervene in a situation early, before it develops into a crisis. Oh, how many stories conclude with a youth leaving home or worse, when by addressing the issue in its early stages, these drastic results could have been avoided!

While it is good to tackle a possible problem as soon as we become aware of it, it is even better to prevent it. It is the same principle as cancer-screening examinations; an ounce of prevention is worth a pound of cure. A suggested prevention strategy is that at least once a month we deliberately talk with our children to see if there are any spiritual or emotional problems developing, any secret sins being harbored. Although this is not an interrogation time and the approach is to be friendly, admittedly, it can sometimes be a bit uncomfortable for both parents and children. Alone with each child, we ask questions, "Is anything on your mind you would like to talk about?" "Is there anything you feel you need to tell us?" "Do you have a clean conscience?" Vague answers, such as "Not really" or "I can't remember," or answers not supported by the body language receive further inquiry. "What do you mean 'not really'?" We always make sure to reassure our children that we really appreciate their openness, and if anything is on their minds, they are always free to come to us. As our Father has said to us, so we can say to our children, "We will never leave you or forsake you" as long as our lives shall last (see Hebrews 13:5).

Step Forward

☐ Review your journal entry for chapter 2. Pray about the best way to bring up your observations.

☐ Refine your planned approach and questions with your spouse.

☐ Today, with the gentleness of a lamb, but in the confidence of the Lord, either bring up some of your observations from the exercise in chapter 2, or give your children a spiritual checkup. Take courage from yesterday's text, "My grace is sufficient for you, for My strength is made perfect in weakness" (2 Corinthians 12:9).

Journal Questions and Answers

1. What was the outcome of the conversations you had with your children today?

_____

_____

_____

_____

_____

_____

_____

_____

2. After your conversations today, list any root problems as you see them and their possible solutions.

_____

_____

_____

_____

_____

_____

_____

_____

_____

_____

3. What have you learned today about yourself and your parenting?

_____

_____

_____

_____

_____

_____

_____

_____

_____

_____

Sin is an expensive business.
—Ellen G. White

CHAPTER 13

Review and Revisit
Section 1

*A man's heart plans his way,
but the Lord directs his steps.
—Proverbs 16:9*

Section 1, "Winning Our Children's Hearts," is the longest and most parent-intensive section of this book. Over the past few weeks, we have been challenged to give our time, money, and energy to our children. We have been called to demonstrate our love by getting to know our children better. While we may not have done everything right, praise God we have done something. It's a sad fact that many parents never spend quality time with their children. If the concepts you have learned thus far have been beneficial to your family, you may want to share them with other parents in need of encouragement.

Today's exercise provides an opportunity to reread and revisit any activities you feel you have not covered thoroughly. And today you also have an important decision to make. Are your children's hearts ready for section 2, "Leading Our Children's Hearts to Christ"? In this next section, we will ask our children either to make a first-time commitment or a deeper commitment to Christ. The ground covered so far has prepared the way for this important step. If, after prayer and discussion with your spouse, you feel you are ready to move on, praise God! If you do not think your children's hearts are sufficiently prepared to ask them to make a commitment to Christ, don't be discouraged. You have a couple of options:

Option 1. Repeat section 1. Please note: repeating these chapters does not suggest that your first attempt was a failure. Not at all! It often takes more time to win one child's heart than it does another's. God has been known to work on people for years before they are ready to make a commitment. We can't expect our children to all progress at the same pace.

Option 2. Repeat only selected chapters. We would suggest these four: chapter 3, "The Results of Affection"; chapter 6, "A Most Powerful Motivator"; chapter 7, "One-on-One, Part 1"; and chapter 8, "But It's Not My Birthday!" This chapter selection is only a suggestion; you know your situation and children best. God will give you wisdom when you ask Him.

What if one of your children is ready to make a commitment, but another is not? Our suggestion would be to take that child who is ready through section 2, calling for that deeper or first-time commitment, then enlist that child's cooperation in helping you revisit section 1 with the other child(ren). Alternatively, include all the children in revisiting section 1. Again, God knows your situation best. James 1:5 tells us, "If any of you lacks wisdom, let him ask of God, who gives to all liberally and without reproach, and it will be given to him."

To evaluate our progress, let's review the key points of section one.

Chapter 1, "What We Need to Succeed"

We commit time to gaining an education or working in our occupation, but what about spending time with our children? Shouldn't we be willing to dedicate time to them too? Chapter 1 helps us build a foundation and calls us to pray for power, commitment, and determination.

How did *you* do? (Circle the appropriate answer.)

a. Skipped it. I did not read that chapter at all.

b. I read the chapter but did not attempt the Step Forward or Journal Questions and Answers section.

c. I read the chapter and did some of the activities but not very many. It was a halfhearted attempt at the activities.

d. I read the chapter and did every activity as well as I could; nothing was left undone. My whole heart was engaged.

How did your children respond?

a. No response

b. Minimal response

c. Good response

d. Excellent (life-changing) response

Chapter 2, "What in Their World Is Going On?"

As children grow up, we often make insufficient efforts to stay connected with their developing world. Unless something changes, a generation gap occurs. Chapter 2 encourages us to become acquainted with our children's world, their rooms, their music, their favorite Web sites, and so on. We were challenged by the admonition in Proverbs 27:23, "Be diligent to know the state of your flocks, and attend to your herds."

How did *you* do?

a. Skipped it.

b. Just read the chapter.

c. Read and did something.

d. Did my best.

How did your children respond?

a. No response

b. Minimal response

c. Good response

d. Excellent (life-changing) response

Chapter 3, "The Results of Affection"

This chapter is based on Ephesians 4:32: "Be kind to one another, tenderhearted, forgiving one another, even as God in Christ forgave you." It emphasizes the powerful effect that kindness, tenderheartedness, and forgiveness have on our children. It also demonstrates how this approach can circumvent the need to correct bad habits after they strengthen.

How did *you* do?
a. Skipped it.
b. Just read the chapter.
c. Read and did something.
d. Did my best.

How did your children respond?
a. No response
b. Minimal response
c. Good response
d. Excellent (life-changing) response

Chapter 4, "Discovering Their Dreams"

Our children have interests and dreams. This chapter urges us to identify those dreams and encourage our children to pursue them. As we relate to our children by taking a sincere interest in what is important to them, we take a step closer to their hearts.

How did *you* do?
a. Skipped it.
b. Just read the chapter.
c. Read and did something.
d. Did my best.

How did your children respond?
a. No response
b. Minimal response
c. Good response
d. Excellent (life-changing) response

Chapter 6, "A Most Powerful Motivator"

Given that everyone enjoys and is motivated by encouraging words, it is a wonder that parents do not use them more often. This chapter emphasizes the value of giving our children proper encouragement and includes practical suggestions to foster a positive atmosphere in the home.

How did *you* do?
a. Skipped it.
b. Just read the chapter.
c. Read and did something.
d. Did my best.

How did your children respond?
a. No response
b. Minimal response
c. Good response
d. Excellent (life-changing) response

Chapter 7, "One-on-One, Part 1"

The value and importance of parents having one-on-one time with each of their children is the subject of this chapter. We are challenged to schedule one-on-one time with each of our children.

How did *you* do?
a. Skipped it.
b. Just read the chapter.
c. Read and did something.
d. Did my best.

How did your children respond?
a. No response
b. Minimal response
c. Good response
d. Excellent (life-changing) response

Chapter 8, "But It's Not My Birthday!"

This chapter discusses the practical follow-up to chapter 4, "Discovering Their Dreams." On this day we actually take a step in fulfilling some of our children's dreams and implement the plans made in chapter 4. It is an important step toward winning our children's hearts.

How did *you* do?
  a. Skipped it.
  b. Just read the chapter.
  c. Read and did something.
  d. Did my best.

How did your children respond?
  a. No response
  b. Minimal response
  c. Good response
  d. Excellent (life-changing) response

Chapter 10, "Invest in the Best"

This chapter introduces the idea and value of regular family time, a planned time in which the entire family can participate in mutually enjoyable activities. Practical suggestions for family activities are included, and parents are encouraged to introduce family time in their homes.

How did *you* do?
  a. Skipped it.
  b. Just read the chapter.
  c. Read and did something.
  d. Did my best.

How did your children respond?
  a. No response
  b. Minimal response
  c. Good response
  d. Excellent (life-changing) response

Chapter 11, "Learning Their Limits"

This chapter encourages us to look at the expectations we have for our children. Are they unrealistic and cause frustration and disappointment, or could we raise the bar higher?

How did *you* do?
a. Skipped it.
b. Just read the chapter.
c. Read and did something.
d. Did my best.

How did your children respond?
a. No response
b. Minimal response
c. Good response
d. Excellent (life-changing) response

Chapter 12, "A Secret Life"

If our children have secret sins in their lives, they are unlikely to make the deeper commitment to Christ called for in chapter 15, "An Invitation." This chapter challenges us to determine whether our children are harboring any secret sins in their lives.

How did *you* do?
a. Skipped it.
b. Just read the chapter.
c. Read and did something.
d. Did my best.

How did your children respond?
a. No response
b. Minimal response
c. Good response
d. Excellent (life-changing) response

Step Forward

☐ Pray specifically that God will give you and your spouse wisdom in deciding whether to move on to section 2 or to revisit section 1.

☐ Review your circled answers above to help determine whether you should move on to section 2 or not.

☐ (Optional) If you plan on moving on to section 2 tomorrow, consider making today a day of fasting.

Journal Questions and Answers

1. What key factors led you to decide to repeat section 1 or continue on with section 2?

_____

_____

_____

_____

_____

_____

_____

_____

_____

2. If you are planning to repeat all or some of section 1, list the chapter(s) you will revisit.

_____

_____

_____

_____

_____

_____

_____

_____

_____

3. If you have some children who are ready to move on and others who are not, what do you plan to do?

_____

_____

_____

_____

_____

_____

_____

_____

_____

Success is to be measured not so much by the
position that one has reached in life,
as by the obstacles which he has
overcome while trying to succeed.
—Booker T. Washington

SECTION 2

Leading Our Children's Hearts to Christ

CHAPTER 14

One-on-One
Part 2

"God so loved the world that He gave His only begotten Son, that whoever believes in Him should not perish but have everlasting life."
—John 3:16

Have you ever told your children the story of Jesus in simple, easy-to-understand language? Do they know the beauty of God's plan to save *them*? As we spend this chapter looking at the account of the gospel, contemplate how you can share this timeless story with your children.

The story of Jesus' birth is well known. Jesus was born in a stable with animals; angels visited shepherds while the shepherds watched their flocks by night; and wise men came from the East, bearing precious gifts. For many, however, the oft-repeated story has lost its significance, being replaced by the festivities of the Christmas season. Think for a moment about what really happened all those years ago. Take the time to visualize each scene.

* * * * *

While in heaven, Jesus enjoyed intimate friendship with His Father, such as only Divinity can comprehend. For as far back as eternity stretches, Their love for each Other had become stronger and more beautiful. Then Jesus, the Commander of the universe, the Creator of heaven and earth, left

His throne of glory and His Father's presence, to come to this dark world, a planet plagued by sin and death. Oh, what a contrast it was! If He had come as a king, born in a palace, it still would have been an enormous sacrifice, but to be born in a barn would have been humiliating. Even though it was probably filled with clean hay, Jesus' first bed on earth was a feeding trough. While today, people seek fame for being the best, the fastest, the richest, the most popular, our God gave up all He had and voluntarily came to earth to live in poverty. Why did He do it? He gave up power and glory and adoration because there was no other way to save *us*, His precious children. He knew that without coming close to humanity, we could never experience the true happiness He longs to give us. Oh, what unselfish love God has for us. What an incredible example for parents!

During His childhood and youth, Jesus lived in Nazareth, a small mountain village proverbial for its wickedness. His parents were poor, and His childhood was simple. His mother was His teacher; and later, He worked with Joseph in the carpentry shop. This brief record of His early life teaches that the quieter and simpler a child's life, the more favorable it is for his or her spiritual development. At the age of twelve, Jesus went with His parents to the temple in Jerusalem and began to realize His mission in life. As He remained at home through His teens and twenties, God was preparing Him for His three and a half years of public ministry.

At the age of thirty, Jesus heard His Father's call to leave Nazareth and go to the Jordan River, where John the Baptist was preaching and baptizing. John announced His arrival. "Behold! The Lamb of God who takes away the sin of the world!" (John 1:29). This began Jesus Christ's public ministry on earth. He turned water into wine, calmed the wild sea, healed the sick, cleansed the lepers, raised the dead, and cast out devils. His sermons were so powerful and His stories so interesting that they caught the attention of vast throngs of people. Jesus thrilled the hearts of the people with His practical, truth-filled messages. Soon He was the most talked-about Teacher in the area. When He spoke, thousands would gather to hear His life-changing sermons.

Unfortunately, His growing popularity caused the other teachers in the temple to become jealous, and little by little, they began to hate Jesus Christ, His messages, and His followers. After a while, the most powerful men in the nation concluded they must silence Jesus' voice, or He would take their place as the leader of the people. They laid plans to kill Him.

Judas, one of Jesus' friends, agreed to help these wicked men with their plans. Leading them to the place where Jesus often prayed, he betrayed Jesus with a kiss. In the dark of night, Jesus was captured and taken to the palace courtyard. Eventually, Jesus was sentenced to death.

As this point in the story, it is worth remembering Jesus could, at any point, have freed Himself. With just a thought He could have called down fire on His persecutors or had thousands of angels fight for Him. But while soldiers cruelly nailed His hands and feet to the wooden cross, Jesus had no thoughts of hurting those who crucified Him.

So why did Jesus allow Himself to be killed? All people have sinned; all of us have broken God's laws. The consequence of sin is death, as stated in Romans 6:23. Jesus died, not because *He* sinned, but because *we* did. His death was for us. "God so loved the world that He gave His only begotten Son, that whoever believes in Him should not perish but have everlasting life" (John 3:16). Will we accept Christ's death on our behalf? Will we say, "Thank You, Jesus, for dying for me! Please give me the power to live for You!"

One day soon, Jesus will come to earth again, not as a baby this time but as a conquering King! Those who have accepted His death and lived for Him will then be fully saved at last, to live eternally with God the Father and our Savior Jesus Christ.

* * * * *

Though simplified, this is the gospel of Christ and the good news of salvation. As you plan a second round of one-on-one time with your children today, may this incredible story make its way into the conversation.

Step Forward

☐ Determine to spend one-on-one time with another of your children.

☐ Review chapter 7, "One-on-One, Part 1." Then plan another special one-on-one time with a different child.

☐ Ask God how He would have you explain the simple gospel story to your child during your one-on-one time today. If appropriate, you may wish to read today's chapter aloud, but don't let the child read the rest of the book!

Journal Questions and Answers

1. Rewrite John 3:16 in your own words, then contemplate the beauty of its message. "God so loved the world that He gave His only begotten Son, that whoever believes in Him should not perish but have everlasting life."

_____

_____

_____

_____

_____

_____

_____

_____

2. Do you think your children have a basic understanding of the gospel of Christ? If not, what can you do to help them understand it?

_____

_____

_____

_____

_____

_____

_____

_____

_____

3. How did your one-on-one time go today?

_____

_____

_____

_____

_____

_____

_____

_____

_____

He [God] has poured out to us
all heaven in one gift.
— Ellen G. White

CHAPTER 15

An Invitation

"Come to Me, all you who labor and are heavy laden,
and I will give you rest."
— Matthew 11:28

When children are committed to Christ, when they have surrendered to the will of God, what unspeakable joy it brings to parents' hearts! True, children will not do everything right, and they still have much to learn, but the contrast between surrendered children and those who are not is significant!

The familiar adage states, If you have your health, you have everything. While health is a wonderful blessing, we suggest an even higher priority. We know parents who would trade everything they have, even health and life itself, if they could see their prodigal children return to the Lord. We suggest that the old adage be rephrased, If we parents are following the principles found in God's Word and we have children who are following the Lord with us, then we have everything! We will use our family as an illustration. We have chosen to follow God and to raise our two children to do the same. The other night, as I was saying good night to my daughter, we began to chat. After a little gap in the conversation, Hannah said, "Daddy, I'm sorry I was grumpy earlier. Do you forgive me?" What price do Christian parents put on such a confession? Yes, the grumpiness itself was only a small thing, but Hannah's asking for forgiveness was so significant. Hannah wanted to tell me she was sorry, and she wanted to be right with God. Praise the Lord!

It is worth whatever perseverance and effort we parents expend to one day hear our children say, "Yes, God, I want to follow You." In the remainder of this chapter, we will explore how to invite our children to make a commitment to God and why our personal testimony of His goodness to us is an important part of this invitation.

Inviting our children to make a commitment to God should not be complicated. If you feel nervous or hesitant about how to make the invitation, don't worry. The Lord has promised to guide us in teaching our children to honor Him.

The previous two weeks of assignments, in addition to drawing us closer to our children, have laid the groundwork for the invitation we are making today. Jesus taught in His parable of the sower, found in Mark 4:1–20, that for a seed to grow and bear fruit, the soil must be good. Accordingly, over the past weeks, we have been working the soil of our children's hearts so that today's efforts are more likely to bear fruit.

The decision we invite our children to make today is a commitment to follow God and live as they know God wants them to. It's that simple. We are actually giving them Jesus' invitation, "Come to Me, all you who labor and are heavy laden, and I will give you rest. Take My yoke upon you and learn from Me, for I am gentle and lowly in heart, and you will find rest for your souls. For My yoke is easy and My burden is light" (Matthew 11:28–30). Children's minds are more literal than adults' minds. So keep your commitment question short, simple, and to the point: "Are you willing to follow God and live the way He wants you to?" Before we ask for this commitment though, we must prepare the way with our own testimony of God's goodness and the benefits of following the Lord.

Our personal testimony of how Christ has helped and is helping us is one of our best tools for leading our children's hearts to Christ. Learning about the inner joy we experience by trusting God, the deeper joy we have in doing things His way rather than our own, along with knowing that He has promised to protect us, is appealing to anyone. Even sharing some of our faults and failings and how we are trying to overcome them can encourage children to make a commitment. If we have failed in certain areas of our parenting, this would be a great time to admit these shortcomings to our children.

As you simply share your testimony of the goodness of God and how you chose to follow Him, keep in mind your children probably do not need as much detail as you may be inclined to give. During family time, or just before bedtime, try to engage your child in conversation about spiritual things, then gently move into your testimony. God will help you to invite your children to make a commitment in a winsome, nonthreatening way. Whether you decide it is better to have this conversation with all of your children at the same time, or one on one, be assured God will guide you and will give you the words to speak.

If your children hesitate or refuse to make a commitment, don't be afraid to ask what stands in their way. Without being pushy, try to find out the reason why they are not ready to make a commitment at this time. It could well be a simple matter that needs only a bit more explanation to clarify. If not, continue to pray, and, if appropriate, ask again in a few days. Perhaps it is time to revisit section 1 or time to take a break for a day or two. Whatever you do, set a date when you will try again.

If your children say Yes to your commitment invitation, be sure to encourage them in their decisions and express your joy and appreciation for them. Invite them to pray a commitment prayer with you. Be sure that you pray first. Thank God for His work in your precious children's hearts, for surely today is a day of rejoicing! Hugs, kisses, and even tears would be very appropriate!

Step Forward

- ☐ Pray specifically that each of your children will take a step of faith and choose to follow God.
- ☐ With your spouse, discuss your approach, testimony, and commitment question.
- ☐ Before the day is over, either together as a family or one on one, ask your children if they are willing to follow God and live as they know He wants them to.

Journal Questions and Answers

1. Explain how you have experienced today's scripture: "Come to Me, all you who labor and are heavy laden, and I will give you rest" (Matthew 11:28).

_____
_____
_____
_____
_____
_____
_____
_____

2. Write your plan to lead up to and ask your commitment question.

_____
_____
_____
_____
_____
_____
_____

3. How did it go?

_____
_____
_____
_____
_____
_____
_____
_____
_____
_____

4. What is your plan now? Will you continue on, repeat section 1, or take a break and start again?

_____
_____
_____
_____
_____
_____
_____
_____
_____

Christ was treated as we deserve,
that we might be treated as He deserves.
—Ellen G. White

CHAPTER 16

A Friend Loves at All Times

A friend loves at all times.
—*Proverbs 17:17*

Today's chapter is structured a little differently. The Journal Questions and Answers section are interspersed throughout the text and are intended to be written as they occur in the chapter.

As we continue to praise God for our progress so far, today we will build on the previous chapter's commitment. Remember though, the road to success is lined with many turnouts, and we need to continue our journey!

Sometimes parents hide behind the excuse, "I came from a dysfunctional family and didn't have good role models for parenting." While having good role models is helpful in knowing how to rear the next generation, they are not essential. We and our children can be a cohesive, happy family even if our family of origin was dysfunctional. Why? Because as Christians, we have God, our heavenly Parent, as our perfect Example and our perfect Role Model!

God has always been available for us. Throughout our childhood He was drawing us to Him with His love and providing for our needs. We may not have always recognized it or accepted it, but that does not change the fact that He is our perfect Parent! So how did He catch our attention and win our hearts? How has He drawn us to Himself? Today, as we explore these important questions, we will learn valuable lessons to pass on to our children.

Now is the time to pull out your pen and answer the following question:

> What things do you appreciate about God, which drew you to Him? Number each point. (Three to six points should be sufficient.)

_____
_____
_____
_____
_____
_____
_____
_____
_____
_____
_____
_____
_____
_____

We will come back to our answers later; but at this point, it would be profitable for us to look at the order of events found in Malachi 4:6, "He will turn the hearts of parents to their children and the hearts of the children to their parents" (NRSV). The *he* in this verse is Elijah or someone with the spirit and power of Elijah (see Matthew 17:12, 13). In the New Testament, Jesus applied this verse to John the Baptist (see Luke 1:16, 17), who prepared the way for Christ's first coming to earth. Today, we are called as God's people to prepare the way for Christ's second coming. But how? Again, God wants to *first* "turn the hearts of parents to their children," and then He will open the way for the turning of the "hearts of the children to their parents."

Sometimes we forget as parents that it is our responsibility to draw our children to us, just as God draws us. It's not just a case of telling them what to do; we have to win their hearts so that they want to do what we ask. God took the initiative with us; we have to take the initiative with our children. Praise God; this is what we have been doing over the past few weeks, which brought us to their commitment in the previous chapter. Now, as we seek to build on that commitment, we must not lose sight of today's scripture: "A friend loves at all times" (Proverbs 17:17).

Let's review our answers to question 1 above in preparation to answer question 2. There we listed several characteristics of God that have drawn us to Him.

How can I be to my children what God is to me? Take each point you listed in your answer to question 1 and realistically plan how you can be to your children in that category what God is to you. Obviously, some things God is to us we cannot fully be to our children, but apply the principle to family situations.

_____

_____

_____

_____

_____

_____

_____

_____

_____

_____

_____

_____

One of the things we appreciate about God is that He is truly "a friend [who] loves at all times." This includes the times when we need correction or discipline. God somehow is able to draw us to Himself while correcting our wayward behaviors. And if we are to be faithful parents, we, too, are going to have to learn to give Christlike correction without alienating our children. It is not true love that says, "I love my children too much to punish them." As parents, we cannot allow our children to grow up to be disrespectful, lazy, or disobedient.

When I [Paul] was eight years old, my parents lived adjacent to the school I attended. I often heard Mrs. Hall shouting at the children on the ball field. She wasn't angry, but it seemed she was very strict. No one got away with anything! I hoped I would never be in her class. But as Providence would have it, at the age of ten, I heard the dreaded announcement: "Paul Rayne, Mrs. Hall." I would be in Mrs. Hall's class the following school year.

Mrs. Hall was strict, and we didn't get away with anything; but today, I can say she was one of the best teachers I had in elementary school. She loved her students enough to correct them! Proper discipline will draw our children to us rather than push them away.

So, how do we maintain a good relationship with our children while administering corrective discipline? Following are seven basic guidelines for effective discipline.

- *Stay calm.* We should not correct our children when we are angry or irritated. This will cause more harm than good. (We will learn more about how to control our emotions in section 3.)
- *Preserve our children's dignity.* We should not humiliate our children by unnecessarily correcting them in front of their siblings or friends. Where possible, call them aside and speak to them privately.

- *Ask questions.* If you were not present when the trouble began, ask questions to ascertain the facts before you address the problem.
- *Keep focused.* Keep your comments brief, calm, and to the point. Long lectures tend to make children tune out the speaker.
- *Pray.* Take time to pray for and with your children, encouraging them to recognize what went wrong and to ask for forgiveness. (There is more about prayer in section 3.)
- *Give consequences for wrong behavior.* God does this with us. If we drive too fast, we get a ticket. If we are lazy at work, we lose our jobs. There should be natural consequences for children's wrong behaviors as well. If one sibling is unkind to another, have him do a job for the one offended. If they use a bicycle without asking, have them clean it. If they shout, have them be silent. Make sure consequences are reasonable and not driven by irritation!
- *Show love.* Even though correction can be hard in the moment for both parents and children, we must show our love for them through the discipline process.

Step Forward

☐ Work toward being to your children what God is to you.
☐ Pray specifically and discuss with your spouse, if possible, ways you can incorporate effective discipline in your home.

Journal Questions and Answers

See below for questions included within the chapter and additional space for answers, if needed.

1. What do you appreciate about God that drew you to Him?

_____

_____

_____

_____

_____

_____

_____

_____

_____

2. How can I be to my children what God is to me?

_____

_____

_____

_____

_____

_____

_____

_____

_____

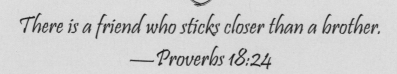

There is a friend who sticks closer than a brother.
—Proverbs 18:24

CHAPTER 17

Review and Revisit
Section 2

We walk by faith, not by sight.
—2 Corinthians 5:7

This chapter reviews and concludes section 2, "Leading Our Children's Hearts to Christ." It has been a practical, hands-on section, covering vital topics and commitments. The next chapter begins our third and final section "Developing Christian Principles at Home."

Chapter 14, "One-on-One, Part 2"

In this chapter, we summarize the simple gospel account of the birth, life, and death of Christ. We are encouraged to make this timeless story a part of our one-on-one time with our children. A correct but simple understanding of the gospel story is essential for children to accept Christ as their Savior. The world conditions us to believe that everything comes with a price and must be earned. Although this maxim may be true in many areas of life, concerning forgiveness and salvation, it is not true. Salvation cannot be earned. We can never perform enough good deeds to gain entrance to heaven. But the notion "If I am good, I will go to heaven" is an easy and obvious trap for our children to fall into.

As we share the gospel story with our children, we should emphasize that God's acceptance of them comes at the beginning of their walk with Him, not at the end. We do not love and follow Him so we can be forgiven but *because* we are forgiven. It is the joy of knowing we are a part of His family that motivates us to live for Him.

Chapter 15, "An Invitation"

We are challenged in chapter 15 to ask our children to make a commitment to God. It can be easy to pass off this responsibility, thinking that someone else—perhaps the pastor or youth leader—is more capable of asking for a commitment than we are, but, as parents, we have more of an influence on our children than we realize. Much of who they are is copied from who we are. We influence their likes and dislikes, their choice of friends, and their worldviews. When our children are hurting, physically or emotionally, they turn to their parents for comfort and support.

Because of our unique relationship with our children, we are the best ones to call them to a commitment to Christ. They may have many aunts and uncles, teachers and friends, but generally children have the closest relationship with their parents. The relationship God chose to illustrate His relationship to us was with that of Father and child. He is not our uncle, grandfather, boss, or even pastor. He is our heavenly Father! If you think you didn't do an adequate job of asking for a commitment, today offers a second opportunity. You can claim God's promise of help:

" 'Fear not, for I am with you;
Be not dismayed, for I am your God.
I will strengthen you,
Yes, I will help you,
I will uphold you with My righteous right hand' "
    (Isaiah 41:10).

Chapter 16, "A Friend Loves at All Times"

The verse quoted in the subtitle leads us to contemplate God's character and particularly those characteristics that have meaningfully touched us. We are then challenged to demonstrate those same qualities to our children.

It is a sobering thought that as parents we hold more influence in the lives of our children than anyone else does. Yet, we are not the only influence. On one side, the devil and his helpers are constantly trying to drag us and our children in the wrong direction. He tempts us by promising ease, pleasure, and happiness. But in reality, he steals from us the real joys of life. On the other side, God is seeking to draw us with His love. He doesn't use force. He doesn't shout at us like the devil does through ads and billboards; but, speaking to our consciences in a still, small voice, He calls us to live nobly. God is "gentle and lowly in heart" (Matthew 11:29), seeking to draw us to Himself, for He knows where true happiness is found.

We also looked briefly at seven basic principles for effective discipline. Although much more could be said on this topic, it's important to learn how to consistently follow these basic principles. Our children need to see that we have their best interests at heart, even when we have to give correction. Like Paul's experience with his grade-school teacher, our children will respect us for our firm, yet loving hand in the future.

Brief introduction to section 3

As we move into our final section, "Developing Christian Principles at Home," we will look at many powerful principles that lead to spiritual growth in both parents and children. So often we fail in our attempts to follow God because we lack an understanding of all the factors involved. Hosea 4:6 tells us, "My people are destroyed for lack of knowledge."

Chapter by chapter, we will unfold the basic principles of practical Christian living. We will not so much list methods as make practical the principles from Scripture. We will explore some of the simple truths Jesus taught and how they can help us personally and as parents. As a result, we will be equipped to make great advances as a family and enjoy a closer walk with God.

Step Forward

- [ ] If there is a child you have not had one-on-one time with, take that opportunity today. As the Lord opens the way, share the simple gospel story with your child.
- [ ] If you feel you didn't do an adequate job of securing a commitment, then seek the Lord for wisdom and try again.
- [ ] Review your notes from chapter 16. Resolve again to be to your children what God is to you. Reread the seven basic guidelines for effective discipline.

Journal Questions and Answers

1. If you had not asked one of your children to make a commitment to follow God until today, how did it go?

_____

_____

_____

_____

_____

_____

_____

_____

_____

_____

_____

_____

_____

_____

_____

2. Explain one way you will attempt to be to your children what God is to you.

_____
_____
_____
_____
_____
_____
_____
_____
_____

3. What is your weakest point when correcting your children? Which of the seven points is more pertinent to you? Why?

_____
_____
_____
_____
_____
_____
_____
_____

Our daily lives are determining our destiny.
—Ellen G. White

SECTION 3

Developing Christian Principles at Home

CHAPTER 18

Soul Power

" 'Not by might nor by power, but by My Spirit,' says the LORD of hosts."
—Zechariah 4:6

When new license plates arrived in the mail, I saw it as an opportunity to teach our five-year-old son how to attach them to the vehicle. We worked together on the front of the vehicle, and then I left him to try his newfound skills on the back. Ten minutes later, I heard angry voices coming from the shop. Upon investigation, I found our then seven-year-old daughter, Hannah, and Caleb physically fighting over the license plate! Apparently, Caleb had asked Hannah to hold the plate while he screwed it in place. Hannah wasn't holding it right, and the holes didn't line up. I'm sure you can imagine the rest.

Walking into this situation, or one like it, can be enough to make parents lose their patience. It is amazing how little patience we have at times. To respond appropriately, we and our children need a power above and beyond our human ability. We need soul power, and this comes only as we all learn of God through personal prayer, studying His Word, and listening to the Holy Spirit. Let's look at each of these areas individually.

Prayer

Prayer can be a little awkward at first for both us and our children when others become aware that we are starting to pray more seriously. But with those initial barriers overcome,

106

prayer soon becomes one of the greatest blessings in life.

Personal, private prayers do not have to be read or recited, nor do they have to be eloquent or lengthy. We can simply talk with God as we would talk with a friend. We can talk to Him in plain, simple language about whatever is on our minds. We can tell Him our problems, our frustrations, our hopes, and our desires, and He will not condemn us or tell anyone our secrets!

It is a mistake to think we have to be "good" before God will listen to us. If this were the case, none could pray "for all have sinned and fall short of the glory of God" (Romans 3:23). Fortunately, we can come as we are and tell Him our faults and failings and ask for forgiveness and mercy. God is "merciful and gracious, longsuffering, and abounding in goodness and truth" (Exodus 34:6). Although God desires us to come to Him as we are, it is important to remember we are mortals, speaking to the immortal God. Prayer is an intimate time, but should not be approached in a casual or flippant manner. As we find a quiet place, and as a sign of respect and reverence we kneel before the Lord our Creator, we can pour out our hearts to Him (see Psalm 95:6). Knowing God has unlimited resources and a heart that loves to give, it is a wonder we pray so little. Prayer brings about a calmer spirit and gives us peace. It is the key in the hand of faith that unlocks Heaven's blessings!

God is interested in even the little things of our everyday lives. We can pray about the things that have to be done when there seems to be no time to do them. We can pray about the nagging burdens that drag us down each time they come to mind. Little by little, effective prayer will have God running our lives, rather than life running us!

In prayer, we can also talk to God about situations that tempt us and cause us to fail. He longs to give us victory in our weak areas. So why shouldn't we ask for strength to resist temptation and to make better choices? If our prayers do not seem to be immediately answered, we must persevere and be sure whatever we are asking is in His will. When our prayers are for spiritual growth and victories over temptation, we can be assured that He will answer.

God's Word

History records the numerous attempts made to silence God's Word, the Holy Bible. It has even been burned in the streets. Although in the past people have been forbidden to read it on pain of death, the Bible has become the best-selling Book of all time! Sadly, the Book that so many gave their lives for is now often ignored, gathering dust on bookshelves. Its wisdom is labeled irrelevant and its principles contradictory or outdated. But dust cannot diminish the relevance of the timeless truth written upon its sacred pages. God's Word is still His love letter to us; it is still the true operators' manual for humankind.

So, how does the Bible help us in our everyday lives? Its help is similar to the way a GPS (global positioning system) navigation system helps us find our destination. The Bible is our guide for navigating life. But in order for us to benefit from it, we must read it! As we contemplate the truths written there, personalize them, and apply the principles to our lives, the Bible will change the way we think and act. Regular reading of the Scriptures will make us better people and better parents, and will bring us peace we have never known before.

Finding time to study God's Word can be challenging, but the study must be consistent to be most effective. One way to ensure that we have the needed time without distractions is so obvious most of us miss it—*go to bed earlier and get up earlier*. It's that simple! Now we have time in the quiet of the morning before the rest of the family is up, to sit at Jesus' feet and learn of Him.

Holy Spirit

The Holy Spirit often seeks to communicate with us, but we must be willing to listen. When we start to feel impatient because our children are fighting over installing the license plate and then we are impressed to remain calm, it is the Holy Spirit seeking to help us in everyday life. When we are about to do something we know is wrong and our conscience whispers, "Don't do it," again it is the Holy Spirit seeking to help us in everyday life.

The Bible describes the Holy Spirit's call to our hearts as a "still small voice" (1 Kings 19:12). It is not a voice that shouts, nor is it a voice we hear with our ears; rather it is guidance we hear in our heart, our conscience. With the call of the Spirit to our hearts also comes the power to make better choices. " 'Not by [our] might nor by [our] power, but by My Spirit,' says the LORD of hosts" (Zechariah 4:6).

Step Forward

☐ Find a quiet place and talk to God about anything that is on your mind. Tell Him your joys and your troubles.

☐ Go to bed earlier tonight, get up earlier tomorrow, and spend some focused time in God's Word. See appendix 1 for suggested devotional Bible passages.

☐ Listen carefully throughout the day and count how many times you hear the Holy Spirit speaking to your heart.

Note: Today's Step Forward does not involve our children. In the next chapter's Step Forward, we will have the opportunity to teach today's lessons to our precious children.

Journal Questions and Answers

1. Expand today's verse into a thoughtful paragraph: " 'Not by might nor by power, but by My Spirit,' says the LORD of hosts" (Zechariah 4:6).

_____

_____

_____

2. How was your prayer time? What did you end up praying about the most, and why?

_____

_____

_____

_____

_____

_____

_____

3. What time are you planning to go to bed tonight? What situations may prevent you from meeting this goal? What are the solutions?

_____

_____

_____

_____

_____

_____

4. How many times did you hear the Holy Spirit calling to you today? How did you respond?

_____

_____

_____

_____

Prayer does not bring God down to us,
but brings us up to Him.
—Ellen G. White

CHAPTER 19

Winning Worship

Give unto the LORD the glory due to His name;
worship the LORD in the beauty of holiness.
—Psalm 29:2

We have all seen advertisements for classes on how to get the most out of Microsoft Word or how to start your own home business; but who ever heard of a class being offered on learning to heed the Holy Spirit? Yet, surely it is important for us and our families to know the practical steps of growing in Christ from day to day! Because such instruction is not widely available, we and our children sometimes struggle in the basics of our Christian walk.

In the previous chapter, we looked briefly at the three major areas relating to Christian growth: talking with God in prayer, reading God's Word, and listening to the Holy Spirit. Today, we will learn how to teach our children these essentials.

Teaching our children to pray

Some have the misconception that praying is easy—you just kneel down and talk to God. Or the misconception that reading the Bible is simple—you just open the Book and read. But that same logic would lead us to wonder why there are courses offered to learn Microsoft Word. Why not just turn on the computer and type? Because, as we all know, using Word was not that simple the first time we tried. For our children to receive the blessings of prayer, Bible study, and listening to the Holy Spirit's guidance, they are going to need a class. And, today, we are the appointed teachers!

When teaching our children to pray, setting an example is our best tool. As our children join us in daily prayer, as they listen to their parents thank God for His goodness and care, asking Him for wisdom and protection, they learn valuable lessons on how to communicate with God. As they hear us talking to God as talking to a friend, asking for God to bless us so we can do our best in resisting temptation, they are being educated by example.

After we have prayed, we should invite our children to pray. Begin with the children that made a commitment during the activity in chapter 15. Have younger children repeat every few words after you. The time immediately after prayer is a great time for a family hug and provides a natural opportunity to tell our children that we love them.

The best time to pray with our children is during family worship. In the morning, before the demands of the day take us in different directions, we should gather our family together in the living room or around the table for a few minutes of prayer and the reading of God's Word. It may sound old fashioned, like something our grandparents did years ago, but, as family worship is established in our homes, it becomes the avenue of religious and moral instruction for the family. It becomes a regular how-to-pray class for our children and an ongoing course in how to listen to the still, small Voice of the Holy Spirit. Family worship should not be a long lecture, but rather something that is interesting and geared specifically to the ages of our children. It should be short and lively, so as to hold the interest of all involved.

A sample format for family worship

Following is a suggested format for family worship.

Open with a short prayer. Ask God to bless this special time. Anyone in the family may open worship.

Read a few verses from the Bible. See appendixes 1 and 2 for ideas. Invite questions from the family or explain the verse and how it applies to family members. Dad or Mom (in Dad's absence) should lead this portion of worship.

Sing. Add this component if you are comfortable singing. It's very enjoyable once you get into it!

Close with prayer. As the entire family kneels, ask the children to pray out loud. Dad or Mom should have the last prayer.

With this special time each day, we have a consistent, regular time for our children's religious education. We have time to teach our precious children to pray, time to hear their sweet voices lifted to God in prayer. A family without worship is like a country without schools (or churches!). No one would dream of such a thing, for surely it would spawn ignorance with all of its woeful results!

Teaching our children Bible lessons

You may feel unqualified to teach your children from the Bible, but as you proceed little by little (which is just what they need), it can be done. Remember, family worship is an ideal learning time. Just ten to twenty minutes, depending on the ages of your children, is sufficient to explain a few verses or read a Bible story. Many Bible lessons and character-building stories appropriate for use in family worship are available for various ages. By spending a little time in worship each day with our children, we can cover all the major lessons in the Bible in three years.

Teaching our children to heed the Holy Spirit

As important as prayer and the reading of God's Word is for us and our children, we must also listen to the Holy Spirit. Unless we learn to heed the still, small Voice of the Holy Spirit through the day, we will find ourselves continuing to struggle in our walk with God. The purpose of prayer and study is to prepare and educate us for the day ahead and to make our consciences more sensitive to what is right and good. Only then can we make wise choices that will bring honor to our heavenly Father. Let us illustrate.

In recent years, our children have developed the somewhat embarrassing habit of collecting coins they find on the floor. It doesn't matter whether we are going through security at an airport or checking out at a store, when they spy a dropped coin, albeit just a penny, they are immediately planning the best way to retrieve it. Recently, while making a return at a local store, our ten-year-old son saw an older lady unknowingly drop a dime as she walked away. This is where the voice of the Holy Spirit came in. *"Go pick up the dime, and give it to the lady,"* said the voice of his conscience. *"Keep it for yourself,"* said the tempter. The blessing of time with God in the morning is that we are more inclined to do what is right when temptation comes our way. Our son quickly picked up the dime, ran after the rightful owner, and gave it back. This is a simple example but one that illustrates a vital point. We must add the *choice* to listen and to obey the voice of the Holy Spirit to our prayers and readings. The woman was so pleased with our son's honesty that she gave the dime back to him, suggesting he buy some candy. Little did she know the smile on his face had nothing to do with candy, but with the joy of having done what he knew was right and adding ten cents to his collection!

Step Forward

☐ Pray today, with your spouse if possible, that God will help you institute family worship time.

☐ Discuss with your spouse how, when, and where you will have family worship.

☐ Using what you have at hand, be it your favorite Bible story or the last few chapters of this book, begin to teach your children about prayer, God's Word, and the Holy Spirit's still, small Voice. (Don't do all three in one sitting! Keep the time short and interesting.)

☐ Research materials you can use for future family worship times.

Journal Questions and Answers

1. Plan your family worship time. Write out your plans for the next three days.

_____

_____

_____

_____

_____

_____

_____

_____

_____

_____

_____

_____

_____

_____

_____

_____

2. What decisions did you make regarding material to use in the future? Did you purchase anything?

_____
_____
_____
_____
_____
_____
_____

3. How was your family worship time? Did your children pray or make any comments?

_____
_____
_____
_____
_____

4. How many times did you hear the Holy Spirit calling to you yesterday? If you forgot to count, try keeping an approximate count today.

_____
_____
_____
_____
_____
_____

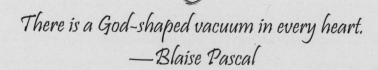

There is a God-shaped vacuum in every heart.
—Blaise Pascal

CHAPTER 20

The Connection That Counts

"I am the vine, you are the branches. He who abides in Me, and I in him, bears much fruit; for without Me you can do nothing."
—John 15:5

In today's world, being connected to a power source is important. A vacuum cleaner does not vacuum until it's connected to power. The fastest laptop in the store will not receive even one e-mail until it is connected to the Web. So it is in the spiritual life. Without a connection to the power of God, we will not operate as we should.

In the New Testament, Jesus used a vine and its clinging tendrils to demonstrate how we are to live the day-to-day Christian life. The illustration is beautiful and so simple and practical that our children can understand it, yet so deep that an entire book would not fully plumb its depths.

Let's look at what Jesus said in John 15:1–8.

"I am the true vine, and My Father is the vine-dresser [grapevine cultivator and pruner]. Every branch in Me that does not bear fruit He takes away; and every branch that bears fruit He prunes, that it may bear more fruit. You are already clean because of the word which I have spoken to you. Abide in Me, and I in you. As the branch cannot bear fruit of itself, unless it abides in the vine, neither can you, unless you abide in Me. I am the vine, you are the branches. He who abides in Me, and I in him, bears much fruit; for without Me you can do nothing. If anyone does not abide in Me, he is cast out as a branch and is withered; and they gather them and throw them into the fire, and they are burned. If you abide in Me, and My words abide in you, you will ask what you desire, and it shall be done for you. By this My Father is glorified, that you bear much fruit; so you will be My disciples."

We will focus on the heart of the illustration found in verse 5 and explore its practical application for us and our children.

In the first few words of John 15:5, Jesus said, "I am the vine." Christ is the Plant, the parent Stock. Each branch needs to be connected to the vine, so it can bear fruit. Similarly, each member of the family needs to be connected to Christ so as to bear "the fruit of the Spirit [which] is love, joy, peace, longsuffering, gentleness, goodness, faith, meekness, temperance" (Galatians 5:22, 23, KJV). John 15:5 concludes, "Without Me you can do nothing." Just as a branch has no access to the life and energy it needs without a connection to the plant, the moment our connection to Christ is severed, we, and the fruit we bear, begin to die.

We must conclude from Jesus' words that every member of the family is dependent on a connection to Christ in order to live a Christian life. Apart from Him, we have no power to resist temptation or to be godly parents or children. How important it is, then, that we know how to connect and stay connected to Christ!

How do we connect to Christ?

Step 1, we come to Christ in prayer, confessing our sins and asking for His forgiveness. In the same prayer, we ask God to give us the gift of repentance. Repentance is the power to turn away from future temptations and to make right, as far as possible, past sins.

Step 2, we must now, while still on our knees in prayer, believe we are forgiven and are connected to Christ, the Vine. We rest our faith on God's words found in John 6:37, which says, "The one who comes to Me I will by no means cast out." We must believe that in God's sight we are now clean and that He can help us to remain clean.

This is how we connect with Christ. Human pride and stubbornness tend to view a relationship with God as complicated. But it is simply by faith in Him as our personal Savior that our union with Christ is formed. Hebrews 11:6 says, "Without faith it is impossible to please Him, for he who comes to God must believe that He is, and that He is a rewarder of those who diligently seek Him." We do not need to do difficult things, such as make pilgrimages or do penance. We just ask Christ to give us His strength. It is that simple. We can ask in faith, and we can help our children do it too!

Now that a connection is formed between the Vine and the branch, between Christ and us, the union must be maintained for fruit to grow. We must learn how to abide in the vine (see John 15:4). By abiding in Him, we will thrive. Drawing our life from Him, just as a branch draws life from the parent plant, we will be enabled to bear the fruit found on the Christian tree: "love, joy, peace, longsuffering [patience], kindness, goodness, faithfulness, gentleness, self-control" (Galatians 5:22, 23).

How do we abide in Christ?

Abiding in Christ is easy to understand, but our human desires and old habits will make it difficult to practice! A person abides in Christ by choosing to trust Christ and to listen to His Spirit. One abides in Christ by repeatedly choosing to obey and do His will. For example, after everyone has left and we notice the sink is full of dishes, abiding in Christ might mean listening to the Holy Spirit urging us to do the task cheerfully, even though it isn't our job. Abiding in Christ might mean choosing not to yell at the children when we find them fighting with each other. As the branch constantly draws the sap from the living vine, so we, through faith, choose to let Christ give us the strength to do His bidding.

As we were making up our family time schedule one day, our children became excited at the thought of sledding down the road that leads to our home. The run is three-quarters of a mile long and can be very fast! We have sledded down the road before and no one has ever gotten hurt, but the potential exists for quite a wipeout. As a mother, I tend to be more aware of danger, particularly if my husband and children exhibit no signs of caution. As we discussed the idea, my son chimed in, "We could do it in the dark, like we did before!" Everything in me recoiled at the thought. I was thinking, *It will be cold, dark, and dangerous. What if a car comes up the road as we are headed down? What if someone gets hurt? What if . . . ?* But deep down in my heart, I knew it would be OK and that God wanted me to join in the simple pleasure of sledding down the road with my family. It didn't have to be as wild as I imagined. In this situation, what did it mean to abide in Christ? It meant to rest in Him, to trust Him, and take strength from Him. It meant giving my fears to Him and taking His courage. Abiding is my choice of faith, and it always brings rest. Praise God, this branch chose to remain connected to the Vine that evening, and through no strength of her own bore the fruit of love, joy, peace, and faith!

Step Forward

☐ Read John 15:1–8. Carefully and prayerfully contemplate each verse and its meaning.

☐ If you haven't already done so, connect to God through prayer. Remember, it is a faith experience.

☐ Choose to abide in Christ today. Let nothing worry you. Give all your troubles to Him and exchange them for rest and peace.

☐ If your children give any hint that they notice a change in you, tell them of the joys of being connected to Christ.

Journal Questions and Answers

1. List anything that impressed you as you read John 15:1–8, and explain why.

_____

_____

_____

_____

_____

_____

_____

_____

_____

_____

_____

_____

_____

_____

_____

_____

2. Did you connect with Christ in prayer today? If not, what is holding you back? How can this obstacle be removed?

_____

_____

_____

_____

_____

_____

_____

_____

3. Were you able to abide in Christ today? What experiences did you go through that either broke or strengthened your new relationship with Christ?

_____

_____

_____

_____

_____

_____

_____

_____

_____

_____

_____

It's not what you know but whom you know.
—Author Unknown

CHAPTER 21

Review and Revisit
Chapters 18-20

When my spirit was overwhelmed within me, then You knew my path.
— Psalm 142:3

Today, we will review the last three chapters, "Soul Power," "Winning Worship," and "The Connection That Counts." We will also draw from the encouragement God has provided in His Word.

Chapter 18, "Soul Power"

Prayer, reading God's Word, and obeying the Holy Spirit's promptings are the only true powers for soul development, for they bring the human in contact with the Divine. Many other suggestions for self-improvement have come and gone. The more recent self-help groups and the notion we have to develop the good within us bring only transitory results. This pull-yourself-up-by-your-bootstraps attitude limits us to human achievements, when the God of the universe, the One who created us and spoke worlds into existence, stands ready to assist us.

The reason we do not experience the fullness of God's power in our lives is that often we do not give ourselves fully to Him. We shrink from following God completely, fearing that so doing may lead to missed opportunities. We think we can skip our morning prayer time or our study of His Word, and no harm will be done. But the truth is, as we miss one

123

day and then another, we start to drift from God. His still, small voice becomes quieter and quieter, until we lose our spiritual union with our Maker. One of the well-known hymns, "Trust and Obey," says it well:

> But we never can prove the delights of His love,
> Until all on the altar we lay,
> For the favor He shows, and the joy He bestows,
> Are for them who will trust and obey.

Oh, how true it is. Children are quick to pick up the spirit of halfhearted devotion. Many teenagers leave their parents' religion because of the hypocrisy they see at home. Our only hope for something better is to spend time with God in the morning and then to obey the Holy Spirit's call to our hearts throughout the day.

Chapter 19, "Winning Worship"

As we lead out in family worship, as we press on in the hard times, praying and working through our weak areas, wonderful results await us. Recently, we received an e-mail from friends we have come to love. The mother wrote, "Seeing our teenage son fully surrendered to the Lord on a daily basis and knowing it might not have been that way causes such joy in our hearts!" These parents would be the first to admit their faults, but they have persevered in training their sons to follow the Lord, and they have sought to lead their children by both instruction and example. God does not have favorites. He has promised to bless all who earnestly seek His help, all who will trust and obey.

Following are just a few of the promises God has given us in His Word. Scripture describes them as "exceedingly great and precious promises," saying "that through these [promises] you may be partakers of the divine nature, having escaped the corruption that is in the world through lust" (2 Peter 1:4).

Take time to read each promise a couple of times. Contemplate the depth of the meaning of each verse and how it applies to you and your family. (See appendix 2 for more encouraging Bible verses.)

- "My grace is sufficient for you, for My strength is made perfect in weakness" (2 Corinthians 12:9).
- "I will instruct you and teach you in the way you should go; I will guide you with My eye" (Psalm 32:8).
- "And you will seek Me and find Me, when you search for Me with all your heart" (Jeremiah 29:13).
- "Train up a child in the way he should go, and when he is old he will not depart from it" (Proverbs 22:6).
- "To him who overcomes I will grant to sit with Me on My throne, as I also overcame and sat down with My Father on His throne" (Revelation 3:21).

Chapter 20, "The Connection That Counts"

As we read God's promises, either in our personal time with God or in family worship, we are encouraging ourselves to abide in Christ. So often in our attempts to follow God, we think about what He wants us to do rather than what He wants to do *for us*. In the previous chapter, we looked at the invitation we have received to abide in Christ. The word translated as *abide* in John 15 means "to remain, to continue to be held, kept continually, to not depart." Jesus invites us to be kept, to be held, to be close to Him all of the time. He wants to be our Friend, our Counselor, and our constant Companion. In His arms, we are safe.

Jesus didn't marry and have children, but He had twelve rough, stubborn, and self-willed disciples to train. He was successful in His "parenting" because He chose to continually abide in His Father and to keep His Father's commandments. These commandments are not restrictive but protective. They save us from the abiding experience. As we keep His commands and teach our children to do the same, especially the ten listed in Exodus 20, we are abiding in His love and enjoy His utmost care. In John 15:10, Jesus said, "If you keep My commandments, you will abide in My love, just as I have kept My Father's commandments and abide in His love."

Step Forward

☐ If you haven't done so already, complete the Step Forward and Journal Questions and Answers for the previous three chapters. This is most important for you and your influence on your children.

☐ If you have completed the Step Forward and Journal Questions and Answers for the past three chapters, take time to read over your comments in the Journal Questions and Answers sections.

☐ Be determined to abide in Christ today and do God's will above your own. Ask Him to hold you close.

Journal Questions and Answers

1. Has your morning time of prayer and study been beneficial? Are you hearing the still, small Voice of conscience more clearly now than a week ago?

_____

_____

_____

_____

_____

_____

_____

_____

_____

_____

2. How are your children responding to having family worship? Has this worship time been profitable for the entire family? Have you ordered or purchased any Bible study materials?

_____

_____

_____

_____

_____

_____

_____

_____

_____

3. Are you still connected and abiding in Christ? If not, what caused you to disconnect? Are you reconnected now?

_____

_____

_____

_____

_____

_____

_____

_____

_____

Whatever is worth doing at all
is worth doing well.
—Lord Chesterfield

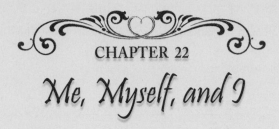

CHAPTER 22
Me, Myself, and I

"With men this is impossible, but with God all things are possible."
— Matthew 19:26

As you step on the bathroom scales, you gasp, "Oh, no! How did that happen?" You are then reminded (we now know it's the Holy Spirit) of how often you have been eating late in the evening and how you have neglected the exercise program you promised yourself you would follow. With teeth clenched and a determination will let nothing stand in your way, you say to yourself, "I mean it this time. I am not going to eat late at night anymore!" You really do mean it. In your mind, you rehearse all the negative effects of late-night eating, as if trying to scare yourself into reform! But a few nights later, after a hard evening with the kids, you somehow talk yourself into believing that just this one time a little bit of the leftover apple pie will not do any harm and will lift your spirits. After finishing the apple pie, a couple of cookies sound good, and before you know it, you are feeling stuffed and guilty. *I did it again! When will I ever learn? There's no hope for me!* Fortunately, there is hope. Read on!

It may not be eating late at night that trips you up, but most of us recognize several areas in which we fail repeatedly. Whether it is shouting at the children, staying up late, gossiping, or wasting time on the Internet, we have to admit we have weaknesses that can undermine our more reasonable intentions.

We are not alone in this dilemma. The apostle Paul, who wrote much of the New Testament, tells us in Romans 7:18, 19, "I know that in me (that is, in my flesh) nothing good dwells; for to will is present with me, but how to perform what is good I do not find. For the good that I will to do, I do not do; but the evil I will not to do, that I practice." This power that works against our efforts to follow God, we call self! It might be useful to consider self as an abbreviation for *selfishness*, and it works in close company with the enemy of our souls, the devil. We all have a self; and as we grow, it grows with us. Who has ever had to take their children to selfishness classes or to teach them to cry when they didn't get their way?

The Bible uses a variety of terms for the selfish part of our nature. Paul calls it the "old man" in Romans 6:6 and Colossians 3:9, our "carnal" mind in Romans 8:7 and 1 Corinthians 3:3, and our "flesh" in Galatians 5:19. While we seldom use these expressions today, we are certainly familiar with the terms *stubbornness, pride, anger,* and *greed*. And the basis of this sinful nature can be described in one word: *self*.

When we are determined not to eat in the evening and grit our teeth to resist, along comes self and knocks us off our feet. It's true that some people have more willpower than others, and they can resist in areas that others fail; but sooner or later, self conquers even the strongest will. This is an area in which God especially wants to help us. As we remain connected with Him, the way a branch remains connected with the grapevine, we receive soul power from Him. Then we are enabled to resist self and the temptations that arise out of it. That is good news, parents, really good news!

So in practical terms, how is self conquered? The first step, which we can do right now, is to recognize and admit that our selfish nature is alive and well. It is easy to identify everyone else's self—but their selfishness is not to be our focus. We must stop blaming our conduct on others. Even if we do not admit it to anyone else, when we recognize self wanting to have its way, we must cry out to God in silent prayer, asking Him for power to overcome.

We want to remember the reassurance that we do not have to overcome all manifestations of self before God will accept us. If we are confessing our sins as we grow, we are accepted as we grow. But God in His love continues to teach His people new ways to serve and glorify Him. The imagery in Proverbs 4:18 can illustrate this growth: "The path of the just is like the shining sun, that shines ever brighter unto the perfect day."

Jesus, the only One who never gave in to self, said, "If anyone desires to come after Me, let him deny himself, and take up his cross daily, and follow Me" (Luke 9:23). Did you catch that? We must deny self in order to follow Christ! We are to count self dead in any actions or decisions of life. Jesus is our Lord, and we follow Him. "Reckon yourselves to be dead indeed to sin, but alive to God in Christ Jesus our Lord" (Romans 6:11).

Our selfish nature is not to be fed, consulted, or obeyed. When we feel hungry and it's ten o'clock at night, self is to be denied by the power of God. We can pray, "God, please give me Your power to deny myself! Lord, You have said You will help me. Please help me. I need You now!" Then we are to remove ourselves from the temptations at hand. Asking God to take away our desire for a late-evening snack as we survey the contents of the refrigerator is not the best plan. Instead, we need to remove ourselves from the source of temptation by leaving the room, drinking a glass of water, or going for a walk. Romans 13:14 admonishes, "Put on the Lord Jesus Christ, and make no provision for the flesh, to fulfill its lusts."

As we teach our children about selfishness, how it operates, and how it is to be denied by the power of God, we must recognize that everyone's strengths and weaknesses are different.

What we find easy, our children may find hard. What one child finds easy to resist, another may struggle with. Be gentle with your children as they learn about how to deny self. Be sure to lead the way with victories over self in your own life.

Step Forward

☐ During your morning prayer time, pray about your self-ishness. Ask God to show you the areas where your self is most prominent. (Look up and contemplate Psalm 139:23, 24.)

☐ Ask God to help you specifically in these weak areas. As you gain victories over self, you will have examples to share with your children as you put into practice what you learn in the following chapter.

☐ Ask your spouse what he or she sees as your most selfish trait. Do not defend yourself!

Journal Questions and Answers

1. List your self's most prominent characteristics. Begin with your most disagreeable selfish characteristic, then the second most disagreeable, and so on.

_____

_____

_____

_____

_____

_____

_____

_____

_____

_____

2. What is causing these manifestations of self to remain alive? What can you do to counteract them or deal with them when they arise?

_____

_____

_____

_____

_____

_____

_____

_____

_____

_____

3. What selfish trait did your spouse bring to your attention? Have you recognized this trait in yourself before?

_____

_____

_____

_____

_____

_____

_____

_____

_____

_____

♡

The warfare against self is the greatest
battle that was ever fought.
—Ellen G. White

CHAPTER 23

A Sword Fight With the Devil

*He answered and said, "It is written, 'Man shall not live by bread alone,
but by every word that proceeds from the mouth of God.' "*
— Matthew 4:4

By now, you probably realize how powerful self can be. It has a way of weaving its way into everything! Whether we want to be the first one to eat or the last one to help, it's simply our self resonating with the tempter's seduction.

But if the devil ever had his sights set on tempting one particular person, it was our Savior! The enemy knew if he could entice Jesus to sin, even once, he would gain control of the entire world with that victory; for there would be no sinless Savior to rescue us. We can safely say that Jesus was the devil's prime target during His thirty-three years on earth!

So how did Christ consistently resist the devil's temptations? Hebrews 4:15 tells us that Jesus was severely tempted to sin. He was "in all points tempted as we are, yet without sin." It is also obvious from this verse that temptation is not sin. Jesus was tempted but was without sin. So how did Jesus, our Example, keep the temptations He faced from turning into selfishness and sin? What did He do that worked every time? The answer is clear, extremely practical, and powerful enough to work for everyone! Jesus resisted Satan's temptations by using the only truly effective weapon in existence—the Word of God.

Notice the event described in this passage from Matthew: "Jesus was led up by the Spirit into the wilderness to be tempted by the devil. And when He had fasted forty days and forty nights, afterward He was hungry. Now when the tempter came to Him, he said, 'If You are the Son of God, command that these stones become bread.' But He answered and said, 'It is written, "Man shall not live by bread alone, but by every word that proceeds from the mouth of God" ' " (Matthew 4:1–4).

Here the devil comes to Jesus, tempting Him to create His own food when hungry. But Jesus had never used His miracle-working power to make life easier for Himself; for He knew the moment that He did, He could not be our perfect Example. Because we cannot turn stones into bread, He wasn't going to either. He came to fight the battles of life as we must fight them, with no advantage over us. So, how did Jesus deal with this temptation? Did He grit His teeth and say, "No, no, I'm not going to do it!" Did He display self-confidence, saying, "You're not going to get Me to fall for that one, you old devil." No, He quoted an Old Testament Bible passage (Deuteronomy 8:3) to the devil, saying, "It is written, Man shall not live by bread alone, but by every word that proceedeth out of the mouth of God" (Matthew 4:4, KJV). It's simple, friends, but it's powerful—and it works! God's Word is a powerful shield that the devil cannot penetrate! The next few verses, Matthew 4:5–10, tell how Satan tried two more times to entice Jesus to use His divine power to benefit Himself, but both times Jesus responded with, "It is written."

Quoting God's Word at the point of temptation has a powerful effect! Have you experienced this power? It is definitely not human power; it is none other than "the power of God to salvation" (Romans 1:16).

The author of Hebrews describes the power of God's Word as a sharp sword. "The word of God is . . . sharper than any two-edged sword" (Hebrews 4:12). The Word of God is a power the devil cannot compete with. But so often, when we fight the devil, we use our own feeble human strength rather than the razor-sharp two-edged sword of Scripture! We can put a lot of effort into gritting our teeth, but the devil is not intimidated. He knows his strength is greater than ours. But when he hears the Word of God, it causes him to tremble and flee!

How do we fight the devil with the Word?

As soon as we are aware that we are under temptation, we must

- Surrender, or re-surrender, our hearts to God.
- Choose, at this very point, to trust God.
- Beat back the devil with passages of Scripture, either in our minds or out loud, if appropriate.

As good and vital as they are, if we follow only steps 1 and 2, the devil will continue to harass and annoy us and, eventually, wear us down. But when we quote the Word of God to him, he has to leave. He has no choice! Sure, he will return with another temptation or maybe even the same one; but we will have won a victory, and we can win the next time too!

If we and our children are to be successful in this sword fight with the devil, at the point of temptation, we must have our weapon close by. This is why David said, "Thy word have I hid in mine heart, that I might not sin against thee" (Psalm 119:11, KJV). Only as we spend time in God's Word, will the Holy Spirit be able to "bring to your remembrance all things that I said to you" (John 14:26).

Remember, Jesus is our Example in all things, especially

in how to be victorious over the temptations of the devil. In every temptation, the weapon of His warfare was the Word of God. It can be ours too.

Step Forward

☐ What is your most common temptation? Find a verse, a "sword," you can use on the devil the next time he comes to you with that temptation.

☐ Use your new weapon, the Word of God, today to fight the devil. Remember to surrender your heart, trust your God, and quote the Scriptures.

☐ In family worship, using Matthew 4:1–10, explain how Jesus fought the devil's temptations.

Journal Questions and Answers

1. Make a list of your temptations and appropriate "sword" texts. Try using www.biblegateway.com or www.bibleuniverse.com to search for texts.

_____

_____

_____

_____

_____

_____

_____

_____

_____

_____

_____

_____

_____

2. Help your children find specific verses they can use when they are tempted.

_____

_____

_____

_____

_____

_____

_____

_____

_____

_____

3. What were the results when you quoted God's Word in your time of temptation?

_____

_____

_____

_____

_____

_____

_____

_____

_____

_____

What we do not overcome, will overcome us.
—Ellen G. White

CHAPTER 24

Organizing Confusion

To everything there is a season, a time for every purpose under heaven.
—Ecclesiastes 3:1

There is no doubt this world is growing "old like a garment" (Isaiah 51:6). Yet some things remain constant. The seasons follow their usual order; the earth's orbit keeps to its predictable path; and the times of high and low tides are so precise that they can be posted at lifeguard stations.

But have you ever stopped to think how life would be without this order and regularity? What would life be like if there were no schedules either in the natural or man-made world? What would a school be like? How would we know when classes were to begin or end? When would the teachers show up, and what would they teach? Also transportation, business, and the whole commercial world would become chaotic without a basic schedule.

In contrast to the predictable schedules of nature and commerce, the schedule maintained by contemporary families at home has become haphazard. We live more like individual entities than united families. We go to bed and get up at varying times, we follow our own spontaneous schedule during the day, we eat when we feel like eating, coming and going as circumstances dictate. The only parts of our lives that are scheduled are often the results of someone else's schedule, whether it be at work or school.

If we were to develop a simple family schedule, we could start synchronizing home life. The result would be a more efficient and predictable use of time. When we allow circumstances to organize our time, we often feel frustrated and not in control.

A little thought about how we use our time can make a huge difference. Rather than rushing out the door because we got up late, then having to come back because we forgot something, implementing a schedule will result in a calmer, more organized, and, ultimately, more enjoyable life. It was Solomon, a man renowned for his wisdom, who said, "To everything there is a season, a time for every purpose under heaven" (Ecclesiastes 3:1).

To make a family schedule, begin with those things that are already set, such as the time the family has to leave for work or school in the morning. From there, work backward and schedule a time when the entire family can assemble for breakfast. Work back from breakfast to determine an appropriate time to begin family worship. Once these three times are established—worship, breakfast, and leaving the house—various family members can decide when they need to get up to have their personal time with God in order to be ready for family worship.

Sample weekday morning schedule

The following is a sample of a weekday morning schedule:

5:00 A.M.   Mom and Dad up, personal grooming, prayer and Bible study

5:30 A.M.   Children up, personal grooming, prayer and Bible study

6:00 A.M.   Prepare breakfast and pack lunches

6:30 A.M.   Breakfast

7:00 A.M.   Family worship

7:45 A.M.   Leave for work or school

This schedule is only a sample. Obviously, it will not work in every home. When you are planning your family's schedule, be sure to build a little extra time into your schedule for those unexpected things that always seem to come up when you're trying to get out the door.

Once we know our rising time, we can determine when we need to go to bed, taking into consideration how much sleep we need. Some people need more sleep than others, and most of us do not get sufficient sleep to maintain good health. Too little sleep leaves us stressed, impatient, and fatigued. Be realistic in estimating when you and your children need to turn in for the night. Most children go to bed later than they should, which prevents them from getting the rest they need.

Interestingly, in the Creation account found in Genesis 1, we are told "evening and the morning" were the first day, second day, and so on. Evening was listed first, then morning second. God intended us to have the rest we need before the day begins, rather than collapsing into bed to recover!

Sample evening schedule

The following is a sample of a weekday evening schedule:

6:30 P.M.	Family time
7:30 P.M.	Family worship/storytime
8:00 P.M.	Children to bed
9:30 P.M.	Mom and Dad to bed

Again, times will have to be adjusted for each home.

So often our family schedules are unwittingly influenced by society. This is especially true concerning the time we go to bed! Our culture is built around late evenings, as people tend to watch television and socialize late into the evening hours. This is no accident! It is by design of the enemy of real happiness. When we go to bed so late that we haven't gotten sufficient rest, we struggle to get up early enough to have a quiet and relaxed morning. Even the thought of a quiet and relaxed morning seems foreign to us. More typically we have time only for personal grooming, and we skip breakfast in order to get out of the door on time. The morning hours, when the day is fresh and unspoiled, are totally missed. But this is just the time when our minds and bodies should be well rested from a good night's sleep so that we can commune and connect with our Creator. Morning is the time to think through our day, to plan our work, and to pray for our children. The morning truly is the forgotten part of the day, that beautiful time with God where true happiness is born. Benjamin Franklin said it simply, "Early to bed and early to rise, makes a man healthy, wealthy, and wise."

Step Forward

☐ Plan a time when you and your spouse can draft a family schedule.

☐ Set a start date for your new family schedule. Consider establishing a regular bedtime for a week, before adding other items to the schedule.

☐ Once you have a schedule planned, run it by your children (as age appropriate) for their input. Remember, parents have the final word.

Journal Questions and Answers

1. Write out a tentative morning and evening schedule for your family.

_____

_____

_____

_____

_____

_____

_____

2. How do you feel about going to bed earlier and getting up earlier?

_____

_____

_____

_____

_____

_____

_____

_____

_____

_____

3. What difficulties do you foresee in following a schedule at home?

_____

_____

_____

_____

_____

_____

_____

_____

_____

_____

Plan your work; work your plan.
—Author Unknown

CHAPTER 25

Review and Revisit
Chapters 22-24

Your ears shall hear a word behind you, saying,
"This is the way, walk in it."
—Isaiah 30:21

Carolyn and I spent some time in Africa in the late eighties. As we drove the eighteen hundred kilometers from Johannesburg, South Africa, to Lusaka, Zambia, we learned how ridiculous self can be. We were experiencing all kinds of vehicle trouble. Our little car, loaded with supplies, repeatedly overheated in the mountain passes. Later, a hose broke, leaving us with no brakes in the sparsely populated African bushland. But it was a flat tire that caused me to lose it.

I was driving faster than I should have been on a potholed road just north of Victoria Falls. Carolyn asked that I drive a little more slowly. It was a reasonable request, but it struck me wrong. I was bent on getting back to our mission station, still another twelve hours away. Moments later, it happened. *Bang! Hiss!* We had hit a deeper-than-usual pothole, which resulted in an instant flat tire. I asked Carolyn to put out the hazard triangle, a law in Zambia. With self boiling below the surface, I began my task of changing the tire. Moments later, I sensed someone watching me. Turning around, I saw Carolyn, just a few yards away, with the triangle at her feet. Self was ignited, and with all of the suppressed tension of the past few days spilling out, I yelled, "Not there!"

My reaction was nothing more than a display of rotten, old self. Shouting didn't make me feel better, and it didn't help get the tire changed. Praise God, we can overcome these responses based on personal feelings and live new lives in Christ.

Chapter 22, "Me, Myself, and I"

As we recognize our self and selfishness and seek to deny it a place in the home, our children will notice and enjoy the difference. They may not verbalize it, but you can be sure they all will be thinking, *Something about Mom and Dad is different, and I like it.*

Leading our children in the right way, rather than pushing them ahead of what we are willing to do ourselves, is foundational to parenting success. It is easy to become angry and raise our voices to a child who is displaying spiteful behavior, but a demonstration of our self will not fix his or her self! Only as we abide in Christ and live out the fruits of the Holy Spirit—love, joy, peace, patience, and so on—will we be an influence for healing in the family. It is important also to recognize that no matter how well we die to self as parents, we can never get the self out of our children. Only God can do that! We can encourage, instruct, and correct. We can lead by example, and we can pray for our children—but only as they choose to respond to God will their selves truly be conquered. The removal of selfishness in our children is the work of grace, not of force.

The battle to deny self, to surrender self, "to be dead indeed to sin, but alive to God in Christ Jesus our Lord" (Romans 6:11) is the greatest battle we and our children will ever fight. But we have the tools—prayer, the Scriptures, abiding in Christ—and we have a Teacher, the Holy Spirit! God has promised to be with us and give us success! "I will never leave you nor forsake you" (Hebrews 13:5).

Chapter 23, "A Sword Fight With the Devil"

God's words have power! God used words to bring this

world into existence. "He spake, and it was done; he commanded, and it stood fast" (Psalm 33:9, KJV). Men may labor for years to construct a multistory building, but God can speak worlds into existence in an instant. This is the kind of power we need when seeking to deny self and to resist the devil. Praise God we have an entire volume of His promises. If we truly surrender self, resist the devil, and quote God's Word when we are tempted, we can gain precious victories!

Unfortunately, we are not as acquainted with Scripture as we should be. Over the years, we have been systematically distracted and, thus, separated from our Source of power. Now is the time to be in God's Word, memorizing passages and promises that will help us in our daily battles with temptation and self. As parents, we would do well to take the time to teach our children verses from the Bible that they can memorize. If they can remember nursery rhymes and children's songs, they can remember Scripture! When our children were three and five years old, a friend gave us a tape of someone singing 1 Corinthians 13, not a shortened version, but the whole thing, more than 280 words! We thought there wouldn't be any way our three-year-old son could remember the entire chapter. But we listened to the tape every day as we folded laundry, and in six weeks, we all had the entire chapter memorized, even our three-year-old! Children's minds are like sponges, soaking up whatever they are exposed to. Rather than feeding them cartoons, let's feed them something that will have eternal benefits.

Chapter 24, "Organizing Confusion"

Scheduling is one of those topics we love to hate. All kinds of objections well up inside of us at even the thought of living by a schedule. Our self recoils at the thought of being "tied down" or "locked in" to a routine. But self always rebels against discipline. Self wants to be free to be late and make others wait, free to take two hours to do a ten-minute task, free to stay up late and skip time with God in the morning. But self will never make us happy. It is as we follow God and apply His principles, one of which is "let all things be done decently and in order" (1 Corinthians 14:40), that we will find life more fulfilling and rewarding.

Once a family schedule has been determined, the next challenge is to live by it. Initially, we encourage you to work on establishing a morning and evening schedule only, leaving the details of the rest of the day flexible. Keep the schedule simple and make sure it is not too tight. If adjustments are needed, and undoubtedly they will be, feel free to make them. But remember if we are trying to fit too many activities into too short a time, no amount of tweaking the schedule is going to work. If your schedule is jam-packed, some activities may need to be removed.

Once we have lived by our schedule for a month, new habits will develop; and it will begin to feel more natural. After two months, we will not be able to imagine going back to the confusion of the past. We have raised our children on a schedule. A few years ago, while building our home, our schedule slipped into last place on the priority list. After three or four months of this kind of living, our children were begging us to "get back on a schedule!"

Why not decide to die to self and give a schedule a try!

Step Forward

☐ Review the Step Forward and Journal Questions and Answers for the previous three chapters.

☐ Catch up on any challenges the Lord is laying on your heart.

☐ Check out the useful Scripture memorizing resources listed in appendix 3.

Journal Questions and Answers

1. Rewrite Isaiah 30:21 in your own words: "Your ears shall hear a word behind you, saying, 'This is the way, walk in it.' "

   _____
   _____
   _____
   _____
   _____
   _____
   _____
   _____
   _____
   _____
   _____
   _____

2. What is the most important thing you can do for your children today?

   _____
   _____
   _____
   _____
   _____
   _____
   _____
   _____
   _____
   _____
   _____
   _____

3. If you are holding back on starting a family schedule, what is stopping you? Be honest.

_____

_____

_____

_____

_____

_____

_____

_____

_____

_____

_____

_____

_____

_____

_____

_____

Man's necessity is God's opportunity.
—Ellen G. White

CHAPTER 26

Building on Success

Being confident of this very thing, that He who has begun
a good work in you will complete it until the day of Jesus Christ.
—Philippians 1:6

In the first chapter, we read how Shackleton and his men persevered, and all of them were rescued. Victory for them meant physical survival. But as we discovered, their ultimate victory consisted of many smaller victories. They abandoned the *Endurance* before it sank, survived blizzards, found food, navigated their way to Elephant Island, and finally arrived at South Georgia Island. One victory followed another until they reached their goal. Similar perseverance is necessary when rearing our children. We need to be continually building on success.

While we haven't had to endure months on Antarctic ice floes in subzero temperatures, the journey through the exercises in *The Connected Family* has required consistent effort. We have been challenged to give time, patience, and love to our children in ways that we may not have done before. We have had hard, stern battles to fight with our own selfishness; and although we have not done perfectly, we have made immeasurable progress. Only time will tell the value of our efforts and the depth of the bonds we have forged with our children during this process. The joy of knowing that we have become better parents should give us a deep satisfaction and put a smile on our faces.

Yet where do we go from here? How can we keep the spirit and momentum begun while studying *The Connected Family*? How can we build on the victories gained and draw still closer to God and to each other? The answer is delightfully simple. We go back to chapter 1 and enjoy its benefits all over again. God will not run out of blessings!

On the first pass through each chapter, we have gained many insights; yet we can go only so deep into the principles and experiences explained. The second time, we naturally will have deeper insights into the material presented, building on our previous experiences. The Christian life, especially as it relates to parenting, is a growing experience. "The path of the just is like the shining sun, that shines ever brighter unto the perfect day" (Proverbs 4:18).

The importance of wholeheartedly engaging in the assignments, rather than only reading the chapters, cannot be overemphasized. Reading through *The Connected Family* without a commitment to its challenges is comparable to planning to learn how to swim without ever getting into the water. It is in the water that we learn to swim; it will never happen on the shore! If you have quickly read each chapter without engaging in the Step Forward and Journal Questions and Answers sections, count your first time through as wonderful preparation. Now the journey can really begin!

For those who have completed the activities, today has the potential to be a dangerous time. Often the greatest victories are followed by the greatest defeats. It is easy to slip back into the old ways, neglecting the children and becoming absorbed in those activities that always seem to demand our attention. It is important that we do not remain satisfied with past achievements but that we stay focused on the goal of making even more progress.

The second time around we want to specifically challenge you to share your experience. There are families you know who would benefit from your experience of drawing closer to each other and to God. Maybe you can think of some now, possibly neighbors, friends, or work associates. Invite them to join you as you go through *The Connected Family* for the second time. By completing your first run through, you have gained the experience and paved the way to be of help to another family. As you and another family or whole groups of families undertake the challenges suggested in *The Connected Family,* your enthusiasm and commitment become catalysts for another family's success. It is only as we share the blessings given us that they multiply.

May God continue to richly bless you, your children, and those you share within the weeks ahead. If *The Connected Family* has been a blessing to you, we would love to hear from you. Our e-mail addresses are carolyn@restoration-international .org and paul@restoration-international.org. We will do our best to reply personally, but until that time, be encouraged and rejoice in the knowledge that "He who has begun a good work in you will complete it until the day of Jesus Christ" (Philippians 1:6).

Step Forward

☐ Thank God for your family and the progress made and victories won.

☐ Determine with God and your spouse when you will commence the next round of studying *The Connected Family.*

☐ Visit www.restoration-international.org to find other resources designed to help today's families.

Journal Questions and Answers

1. Rewrite Philippians 1:6 in your own words: "Being confident of this very thing, that He who has begun a good work in you will complete it until the day of Jesus Christ."

_____

_____

_____

_____

_____

_____

_____

_____

_____

_____

_____

_____

2. What do you consider the most valuable progress made during your study of *The Connected Family*?

_____

_____

_____

_____

_____

_____

_____

_____

_____

_____

_____

_____

_____

3. What is your plan now? Whom will you invite to join
   you, and when will you start?

   _____

   _____

   _____

   _____

   _____

   _____

   _____

   _____

   _____

   _____

   _____

   _____

   _____

   _____

   _____

*Success depends not so much on talent
as on energy and willingness.*
—Ellen G. White

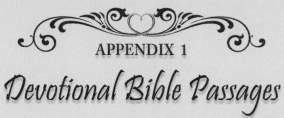

APPENDIX 1

Devotional Bible Passages

Old Testament

1 Samuel 1; 2:1–21 .... Hannah's devotion
Psalm 23 .... Our Good Shepherd
Psalm 27 ....Our salvation
Psalm 51 ....A clean heart
Psalm 91 .... Safe in His care
Proverbs... Wisdom for all
Isaiah 53 ....Our Savior

New Testament

Matthew 5:1–21 .... The Beatitudes
Matthew 13:18–32 .... The sower
Matthew 14:22–31 .... Peter walks on water
Mark 5:22–43 ....Jairus's daughter
Mark 7:24–30 .... One mother's faith
Luke 6:46–49 ....Wise and foolish builders
Luke 9:10–17 .... Feeding the five thousand
Luke 15:3–7 ....The lost sheep
Luke 15:11–32..The prodigal son
John 3:1–21 ....Born again
John 11:1–46 .... Lazarus raised
John 15 .... Abiding in Jesus
Acts 9:1–22 ....Saul becomes Paul
Acts 12:1–19............................Peter delivered from prison
1 Corinthians 13...................................... The love chapter
Hebrews 11 ....Faith
James .... Patience, faith, and wisdom
1 John 3 and 4 ....Love for God and man

APPENDIX 2

Encouraging Bible Verses

Proverbs 3:5, 6

Trust in the LORD with all your heart, and lean not on your own understanding; in all your ways acknowledge Him, and He shall direct your paths.

Philippians 4:19

And my God shall supply all your need according to His riches in glory by Christ Jesus.

Psalm 37:3–5

Trust in the LORD, and do good; dwell in the land, and feed on His faithfulness. Delight yourself also in the LORD, and He shall give you the desires of your heart. Commit your way to the LORD, trust also in Him, and He shall bring it to pass.

Isaiah 40:11

He will feed His flock like a shepherd; He will gather the lambs with His arm, and carry them in His bosom, and gently lead those who are with young.

Galatians 6:9

And let us not grow weary while doing good, for in due season we shall reap if we do not lose heart.

Proverbs 22:6

Train up a child in the way he should go: and when he is old, he will not depart from it.

Isaiah 54:13

All your children shall be taught by the LORD, and great shall be the peace of your children.

Isaiah 49:25

Even the captives of the mighty shall be taken away, and the prey of the terrible be delivered; for I will contend with him who contends with you, and I will save your children.

Philippians 4:13

I can do all things through Christ who strengthens me.

Psalm 32:8

I will instruct you and teach you in the way you should go; I will guide you with My eye.

James 1:5

If any of you lacks wisdom, let him ask of God, who gives to all liberally and without reproach, and it will be given to him.

Isaiah 65:24

It shall come to pass that before they call, I will answer; and while they are still speaking, I will hear.

Matthew 21:22

And whatever things you ask in prayer, believing, you will receive.

Psalm 27:14

Wait on the LORD; be of good courage, and He shall strengthen your heart; wait, I say, on the LORD!

2 Corinthians 5:17

Therefore, if anyone is in Christ, he is a new creation; old things have passed away; behold, all things have become new.

John 13:34

A new commandment I give to you, that you love one another; as I have loved you, that you also love one another.

Isaiah 30:21

Your ears shall hear a word behind you, saying, "This is the way, walk in it," whenever you turn to the right hand or whenever you turn to the left.

1 Peter 5:7

Casting all your care upon Him, for He cares for you.

John 14:27

Peace I leave with you, My peace I give to you; not as the world gives do I give to you. Let not your heart be troubled, neither let it be afraid.

Romans 8:28

And we know that all things work together for good to those who love God, to those who are the called according to His purpose.

Matthew 6:33

But seek first the kingdom of God and His righteousness, and all these things shall be added to you.

John 13:34, 35

A new commandment I give to you, that you love one another; as I have loved you, that you also love one another. By this all will know that you are My disciples, if you have love for one another.

APPENDIX 3

Resources

Restoration International
www.restoration-international.org
888.446.8844

The offical Web site of Paul and Carolyn Rayne's full-time ministry. View their speaking schedule, browse available CDs, MP3s, and DVDs on marriage, family, and the personal Christian walk.
Authors e-mail addresses:
paul@restoration-international.org or
carolyn@restoration-international.org.

The Connected Family companion Web site
www.theconnectedfamily.info

Watch the television series based on *The Connected Family* book.

Three Angels Broadcasting Network
www.3abn.org

International Christian television and radio.

Thy Word Creations
www.thywordcreations.com

Dedicated to help parents and children memorize Scripture.

Feeding His Lambs
www.feedinghislambs.com

Resources for parents with young children.

Bible Universe
www.bibleuniverse.com

A complete Bible resource, including Bible school for all ages.

Parenting Boot Camp
by Dr. Kay Kuzma

At last! A short, simple, to the point, basic training manual for parents. Cutting the umbilical cord doesn't make you an informed, capable, and effective parent any more than enlisting in the army makes you a soldier. It's boot camp that trains you for peak performance, so you can make informed decisions and be successful at your mission. That's why every parent needs Dr. Kay Kuzma's *Parenting Boot Camp*.

Paperback, 192 Pages
ISBN 13: 978-0-8163-2377-7
ISBN 10: 0-8163-2377-1

God With Us
God for Us
by James W. Gilley

In his down-to-earth style, Jim Gilley handles the timeless truths from John's Gospel in ways that touch our lives in the twenty-first century. His personal stories from life experiences make John's picture of the Divine Jesus come alive. In these books, we see Jesus Christ revealed as God in the flesh, and you will realize that everything Jesus did, He did for you. And you will be drawn to receive Him into your own heart as your personal Savior.

Paperback, 160 Pages each
God With Us:
ISBN 13: 978-08163-2285-5
ISBN 10: 0-8163-2285-6
God for Us:
ISBN 13: 978-08163-2426-2
ISBN 10: 0-8163-2426-3

Pacific Press®
Publishing Association
"Where the Word Is Life"

Three ways to order:

1	Local	Adventist Book Center®
2	Call	1-800-765-6955
3	Shop	AdventistBookCenter.com